Memento Mori

AN ADVENT COMPANION ON THE LAST THINGS

By Sr. Theresa Aletheia Noble, FSP

Pauline
BOOKS & MEDIA

BOSTON

Library of Congress Control Number: 2021938335
CIP data is available.

ISBN 10: 0-8198-5044-6
ISBN 13: 978-0-8198-5044-7

Many manufacturers and sellers distinguish their products through the use of trademarks. Any trademarked designations that appear in this book are used in good faith but are not authorized by, associated with, or sponsored by the trademark owners.

Scripture texts in this work are taken from the *New American Bible, Revised Edition* © 2010, 1991, 1986, 1970, Confraternity of Christian Doctrine, Washington, D.C., and are used by permission of the copyright owner. All rights reserved. No part of the *New American Bible* may be reproduced in any form without permission in writing from the copyright owner.

Excerpts from the English translation of the *Catechism of the Catholic Church* for use in the United States of America, copyright © 1994, United States Catholic Conference, Inc. —Libreria Editrice Vaticana. Used with permission.

Excerpts from papal magisterium texts © Libreria Editrice Vaticana, Città del Vaticano. All rights reserved. Used with permission.

Excerpts from *The Collected Works of Edith Stein* vol. 4 by Washington Province of Discalced Carmelites, ICS Publications, 2131 Lincoln Road, N.E., Washington, D.C., 20002–1199 U.S.A. www.icspublications.org. Used with permission.

Cover art and design by Sr. Danielle Victoria Lussier, FSP

"P" and PAULINE are registered trademarks of the Daughters of St. Paul.

Published by Pauline Books & Media, 50 Saint Pauls Avenue, Boston, MA 02130-3491

Printed in Korea.

www.pauline.org

Pauline Books & Media is the publishing house of the Daughters of St. Paul, an international congregation of women religious serving the Church with the communications media.

1 2 3 4 5 7 8 9   26 25 24 23 22 21

For Mary Ellen Shea Clifford, my beloved aunt
without whom this book would not exist.
Rest in peace Aunt ME.

In gratitude to all those whose generosity and support
has made this book possible, especially:

Jeffrey Matthews
Ernest Inman
Patricia Judge
Joseph Nelson
Chimène St. Amant
Maria del Carmen Vega
Scott

AUTHOR'S NOTE

Originally this Advent companion began with a short story that centered around an actual event that happened to me and a group of sisters. The story described an incident in which a young man, upon seeing a group of religious sisters out in public, tried to pose for a picture in front of us shirtless and with a fan of money in his hands. When confronted for his inappropriate behavior, his excuse was, "Gotta get the likes man, gotta get the likes." His actions were offensive, but the incident stuck with me because it seemed a perfect analogy of the battle of grace and sin in the soul. In the story, the young man's actions represented the personification of concupiscence.

Though the story could not appear in this book, I would like to share why I thought it important. The Last Things are topics that defy safe, comfortable presentations of the faith and invite a more poetic contemplation of themes beyond our full comprehension. For this reason, unlike my past books on *memento mori*, here I have avoided more didactic, catechetical phrasing, in order to encourage readers to contemplation. So, I originally hoped to begin with a short story because fiction encourages us to enter a poetic world and leave behind safe, black-and-white lines and facile understanding. I continue to believe this book will facilitate

Vanitas Still Life, Herman Henstenburgh (ca. 1700s).

that process in many ways—in great part because of the incredible art that so many artists have generously contributed. My hope is that the writing, art, and prayer prompts will exercise the muscles of your hearts and help you to enter into contemplating the Last Things in ways that resist anodyne presentations. God is found in this journey of mystery and trust, and I have faith that he will bring you there as you travel with this Advent companion.

For all that is in the world, sensual lust, enticement for the eyes, and a pretentious life, is not from the Father but is from the world. Yet the world and its enticement are passing away. But whoever does the will of God remains forever.

— 1 John 2:16–17

Christianity will always be seen by this world as a living paradox, a madness for some, a scandal for others. For us it is a divine truth and reality . . . to sacrifice one's life in order to save it; to lose everything to gain everything. And the peak of the paradox is that poverty becomes wealth; abasement, exaltation; virginity, motherhood; slavery, freedom; sacrifice, beatitude . . . death, life.

— Blessed James Alberione

CONTENTS

MEMENTO MORI,
THE LAST THINGS, AND ADVENT

Memento mori or "remember your death" is a phrase long associated with the practice of remembering the unpredictable and inevitable end of one's life. Popular in medieval times, this tradition stretches back to the very beginning of salvation history for Christians. After the first sin, God reminds Adam and Eve of their mortality: "You are dust, / and to dust you shall return" (Gn 3:19). God's words continue to echo throughout Scripture, reminding readers of life's brevity while exhorting them to remember their death. The Book of Sirach urges, "In whatever you do, remember your last days, / and you will never sin" (7:36). The psalmist prays, "Teach us to count our days aright, / that we may gain wisdom of heart" (Ps 90:12). In the New Testament, Jesus exhorts his disciples to pick up their crosses daily and to remember their death as they follow him to the Place of the Skull: "If anyone wishes to come after me, he must deny himself and take up his cross daily and follow me" (Lk 9:23).

The phrase *memento mori* has been used for millennia in the Christian tradition in reference to reminders of death and the practice of meditation on death. In contemporary pop culture, it still appears, including in YouTube videos, TV shows, and podcasts. It's important to bear in mind, however, that the phrase can be used in many different, and, at times, conflicting ways. In fact, in contemporary usage *memento mori* sometimes means precisely the opposite of what it means in the Christian tradition. *Memento mori* without the Christian sense can be equated with the unfortunate modern acronym YOLO or "you only live once": the idea that we should fit in as much pleasure, money earning, and success as possible before we die. Of course, if one does not believe in God and the afterlife, it might make sense to live according to *memento mori* in this hedonistic sense. If as Christians, however, we truly believe what we profess, we should avoid approaching life according to such a philosophy.

For Christians, death is illuminated by the hope that comes to us through the life, death, and resurrection of Jesus Christ. Unfortunately, many of us nevertheless approach life with mindsets that do not reflect a Christian understanding of death, and thus life. I know this from experience. A former atheist, I entered the convent after a radical conversion experience that changed the course of my life completely. Even after converting, entering the convent, studying theology and philosophy for years, praying regularly, and reading extensively about the faith, I still thought in many ways like an atheist. When I was feeling particularly honest with myself, I had to admit that my priorities, thoughts, and concerns just had not changed fundamentally, even though I was living for Jesus.

Unfortunately, many Christians today, even those fighting to practice their faith and live virtuously, have similar experiences. Swimming in a milieu of postmodernism, deconstructionism, and the ensuing existentialist angst, we naturally find it difficult to center our faith lives in the proper context—in the reality that our life on this earth both will end and is not the end. Combine our modern zeitgeist with how meditation on the Last Things has fallen out of favor in recent decades in the Church, and many Christians find themselves without a deep sense of the meaning of their lives. In fact, many baptized Christians live rather aimlessly without realizing that our Baptism calls us to struggle against concupiscence, an inclination to sin that remains in us even after Baptism. The practice of *memento mori*, or meditation on all of what are called "the Last Things"—death, judgment, hell, and heaven—has been a long, time-honored practice that used to help Christians discover the true meaning of life and fight our concupiscence. Reviving this practice can help us live our lives in a context that continually brings us back to what is most fundamentally important.

Advent might seem like a liturgical season associated more with the joyful anticipation of Christmas than meditation on death and the other Last Things. But just as no days exist in which a human does not die, there need not be liturgical breaks from remembrance of death. Also, in times past, Advent was recognized as the perfect time to take a hard look at all the Last Things. In fact, it used to be the tradition in some parishes that sermons would be given on each of the Last Things to correspond to the four Sundays of Advent. The loss of this traditional meditation on the Last Things during Advent is a sign that in modern times we have difficulty simultaneously holding the challenging and joyous truths of our faith. Advent is both a time of joyful anticipation and sober preparation. The powerful, paradoxical truth of the Catholic faith demands that we keep these truths in tension.

Advent would mean nothing if Jesus did not come to save us from death, humanity's most intimidating enemy and impossible adversary. Jesus was born to die. Through his life, death, and resurrection, Jesus brought us life. And through opening the gates of heaven, he saved us from hell. All this might seem obvious, but it's crucial, no matter how many years we've been Christians or how practiced we are at the faith, to approach meditation on the Last Things with the humble assumption that none of us live fully according to the proper context of the afterlife.

Our faith involves a struggle to learn to desire only Jesus. As human beings, we are prone to distraction and becoming lost in the passing things of this world. We likely experience this every Advent when, amid a liturgical season that invites us to enter into silent awe, shining lights and tinsel vie for our attention. But this is precisely why meditating on the Last Things during Advent can be so spiritually fruitful. Of the many beneficial ways to celebrate Advent, meditating on the Last Things trains us to recognize what is truly important: God. Hans Urs von Balthasar wrote, "God is the 'last thing' of the creature. Gained, he is heaven; lost, he is hell; examining, he is judgment; purifying, he is purgatory." Meditating on the Last Things is completely centered on the God who has come to us in human flesh through the Incarnation and who also will come again at the moment of our death and at the end of the world. Throughout this Advent and even after Christmas celebrations arrive, may we remember our inevitable death and continue to prepare.

 Memento mori,
Sr. Theresa Aletheia Noble, FSP

HOW TO USE THIS COMPANION

Memento mori, or remembering death, judgment, hell, and heaven, is a deeply personal practice that can bring complex emotions to the surface. For this reason, it's important to thoughtfully integrate *memento mori* into your spiritual life. To aid you in this journey, this companion has daily prompts for journaling and prayer. You may find it helpful to use *Remember Your Death: Memento Mori Journal* for your reflection and journaling when you respond to these prompts. At the top of each page of the journal is included a *memento mori* quote from Scripture, Church Fathers, or the saints. Whether you use the journal or not, it would be helpful to respond to the daily prompts in this companion in order to integrate this practice into your life on a deeper level. *Memento Mori: Prayers on the Last Things* is another resource that you can pray with as you use this Advent companion. The prayer book includes introductions to each of the Last Things as well as prayers and practices that you can incorporate into your prayer life.

Also, it's important to note that this Advent companion can be used for several Advents. Don't feel like a failure if you are unable to read it every day. Do what you can, and God's grace fills in the gaps. In fact, that is the point of this practice. *Memento mori* is centered on God's grace, not our abilities. Regular remembrance of death is not about being perfect, healthy, and strong (see Ps 73). Rather, we remember our death in order to remember our weakness. We are frail sinners in need of a Savior, and the Incarnation is a demonstration and celebration of God's strength, not ours.

As you integrate *memento mori* into your life, you may find more fruit in the practice if you are able to connect with those in the community of the Church who are on the same journey. Death is the fate of every human being, but as Christians we also share the hope of eternal life. Together on life's journey, we can help one another to keep both our death in mind and our eyes on Jesus. So consider talking with family and close friends about your journey, ask for their feedback, and invite them to join you. You can share your reflections and responses with the wider online community with the hashtags #mementomori and #livememento-mori. I also encourage you to connect online with the artists who have contributed much of the art in this book, which would not be the same without it.

Memento Mori Skull Symbolism

Resurrection
BUTTERFLY

Victory
LAURELS

Death
SKULL

Humanity
FALLEN LAURELS

First Week of Advent

DEATH

Adventus, the Latin word from which the word "advent" is derived, means "coming" or "arrival." And indeed, during this season we remember a variety of ways that God comes into our lives. He comes to us in the Incarnation; he comes to us in Baptism; he comes to us throughout the day, even when we do not take notice; he comes to us at the end our lives in the moment of our death; and he will come to us at the Second Coming at the end of the world. These are the most important arrivals ever to occur, both in our individual lives and in the entire world. We know this deep down, and we also know that we must prepare for these arrivals. Still, during the season of Advent, the preparation of Christmas cards, parties, and gifts often overtakes our immediate attention. Even when we try to live Advent by preparing to welcome Baby Jesus, our efforts easily can become distracted by overly sentimental or secularized aspects of the season.

If we avoid living Advent on a deep spiritual level, it might be because we want to forget the difficult truth that death is waiting for us. Forgetfulness of death is a consequence of original sin that pervades every day of our lives and clouds many of our decisions. But whether we ignore it or not, death will come, so we must be ready. Our life as baptized Christians is not an easy walk; it's a run, a struggle (see Heb 12:1). And our noble baptized souls, in which God has come to dwell, deserve the dignity and benefits derived from regular meditation on death. For this reason, for many centuries the Christian tradition has emphasized the pious practice of regular meditation on death as an aid in our struggle to live our baptismal graces.

During Advent, when we meditate on the first coming of Christ, the mystery of the Incarnation, we remember also how the Son of God humbled himself and took on human flesh in order to defeat death through his own death. When we meditate on the death of Christ, we may tend to focus mostly on the Cross. But Jesus began to die the moment he came to earth. The divine humiliation of the Incarnation began in the union of the divine nature with feeble human nature, which tends toward death, in the one person of Jesus Christ. By taking on human nature, the Son of God defeated humanity's greatest foe—permanent death in sin. This is a glorious mystery, a joyful mystery, an astounding mystery!

Meditation on death during Advent allows us to enter deeply into the true meaning of this holy season, the coming in time of the only One who saves us from death. Unfortunately, the world has no patience for long waits, penitential previews, and hushed liturgical seasons that encourage us to silence and meditation. Glitzy Christmas lights appear and parties begin often far before Advent is over, and before we know it, we are catapulted through Advent preparation into Christmas joy. But we cannot truly experience the joy of Christmas without first entering the quiet of Advent. This season calls us to remember that just as death did not spare the Son of God, it will not spare us either. Every person, whether rich or poor, young or old, believer or nonbeliever, is invited to make a choice in life: to ignore death and pretend that life will go on forever or to face death's inevitability. And if we do not accept this invitation to face death now, when will we have another opportunity?

> Death is the end of earthly life. Our lives are measured by time, in the course of which we change and grow old and, as with all living beings on earth, death seems like the normal end of life. That aspect of death lends urgency to our lives: remembering our mortality helps us realize that we have only a limited time in which to bring our lives to fulfillment:
>
> > Remember also your Creator in the days of your youth . . . before the dust returns to the earth as it was, and the spirit returns to God who gave it [Eccl 12:1, 7].
>
> Death is a consequence of sin. The Church's Magisterium, as authentic interpreter of the affirmations of Scripture and Tradition, teaches that death entered the world on account of man's sin. Even though man's nature is mortal, God had destined him not to die. Death was therefore contrary to the plans of God the Creator and entered the world as a consequence of sin. "Bodily death, from which man would have been immune had he not sinned" is thus "the last enemy" of man left to be conquered [*Gaudium et Spes*, 18 § 2].

Death is transformed by Christ. Jesus, the Son of God, also himself suffered the death that is part of the human condition. Yet, despite his anguish as he faced death, he accepted it in an act of complete and free submission to his Father's will. The obedience of Jesus has transformed the curse of death into a blessing.

Because of Christ, Christian death has a positive meaning: "For to me to live is Christ, and to die is gain" [Phil 1:21].

— Catechism of the Catholic Church (nos. 1007–1010)

Memento Mori, Arienda Tankou, @thegoodsheperd_illustrations.

First Sunday of Advent

Year A: Is 2:1–5 / Ps 122:1–2, 3–4a, 4b–5, 6–7, 8–9 / Rom 13:11–14 / Mt 24:37–44
Year B: Is 63:16b–17, 19b; 64:2–7 / Ps 80:2–3, 15–16, 18–19 / 1 Cor 1:3–9 /
  Mk 13:33–37
Year C: Jer 33:14–16 / Ps 25:4–5, 8–9, 10, 14 / 1 Thes 3:12–4:2 / Lk 21:25–28, 34–36

"Stay awake! For you do not know on which day your Lord will come."

— Matthew 24:42

"May he not come suddenly and find you sleeping. What I say to you, I say to all: 'Watch!'"

— Mark 13:36–37

"They will see the Son of Man coming in a cloud with power and great glory. But when these signs begin to happen, stand erect and raise your heads because your redemption is at hand."

— Luke 21:27–28

THE GOSPELS THIS FIRST Sunday of Advent remind us that Jesus will come again at the end of the world. During Advent we recall the coming of Christ both in the Incarnation and in the Second Coming. These themes, so often forgotten in modern Christian life, were central for the

The Fruit of Sin, Tisa Muico, @tisamuico.

early Christians. In a discourse attributed to Saint Hippolytus on the end of the world, he writes, "Through the scriptures we are instructed in two advents of the Christ and Savior. The first after the flesh was in humiliation, because he was manifested in lowly estate. Then his second advent is declared to be in glory; for he will come from heaven with power, and angels, and the glory of his Father."

Christians have been contemplating the advent of Jesus in the Incarnation and waiting for the advent of Jesus in his Second Coming for two thousand years now—but it seems as if our modern world no longer has tolerance for what this requires. Nowadays we rarely recall our inevitable death, let alone the second coming of Christ. But if we don't prepare for death, how can we hope to be prepared for Jesus' second coming? After all, we don't even know for sure which will come first. Are we ready for both? Are we vigilant? Are we awake? If we're honest, we'll admit that while we want to be ready, drowsiness sets in every day. We regularly turn our mind from things of heaven to set our eyes on passing things. We do this in almost every aspect of our lives. To be distracted and drowsy is the state of sinful humanity.

When we near the danger of the death of sin, however, the fire of our Baptism can wake us up. Just when our eyes close, heavy with sleep, the heat of grace will try to awaken us with its warm glow in our souls. The fiery grace of our Baptism, inflamed by the grace of the Eucharist and confession, continually helps us to stay awake. The baptismal indwelling of the Trinity within us reminds us of the inevitability of death and the need to die in Christ so that we might rise with him. Jesus was born to give us the gift of salvation. May we trust in Jesus not to allow us to fall asleep while tending this precious baptismal fire within us. Dear Jesus, wake us up!

Examen *(see p. 153)*

What an impenetrable mystery death is! Yet, at the same time, how simple for the soul that has lived in faith, for those who "look not to what is seen but to what is unseen; for what is seen is transitory, but what is unseen is eternal" (see 2 Cor 4:18). Saint John, whose pure soul was radiant with divine light, gives in a few words what seems to me a most beautiful definition of death: "Jesus knew that his hour had come to pass from this world to the Father" (Jn 13:1). Is not the simplicity of these words touching?

When the final hour sounds for us, we must not suppose that when God comes before us to judge us, we shall remain for all eternity in the state in which God finds us then and our degree of grace will be our degree of glory. By the fact of being delivered from the body, the soul can see him without a veil within itself, as it has possessed him all its lifetime, though unable to contemplate him face to face. This is perfectly true; it is theology. Is it not a comfort to think that he who is to be our Judge dwells within us throughout our miseries, to save us and to forgive our sins?

— Saint Elizabeth of the Trinity, *The Praise of Glory*

Journaling and Prayer

Reflect on how you have tended the fire of your Baptism: perhaps a specific time when the grace of your Baptism helped you to navigate a situation, and another time when the fire of your Baptism was left untended. What happened in each situation? How can you better tend the fire of your Baptism now?

First Monday of Advent

READINGS: Is 2:1–5 (or Is 4:2–6 YEAR A) / Ps 122:1–2, 3–4b, 4cd–5, 6–7, 8–9 / Mt 8:5–11

When [Jesus] entered Capernaum, a centurion approached him and appealed to him, saying, "Lord, my servant is lying at home paralyzed, suffering dreadfully." He said to him, "I will come and cure him." The centurion said in reply, "Lord, I am not worthy to have you enter under my roof; only say the word and my servant will be healed. For I too am a person subject to authority, with soldiers subject to me. And I say to one, 'Go,' and he goes; and to another, 'Come here,' and he comes; and to my slave, 'Do this,' and he does it." When Jesus heard this, he was amazed and said to those following him, "Amen, I say to you, in no one in Israel have I found such faith."

— MATTHEW 8:5–10

IN TODAY'S GOSPEL JESUS is amazed at the faith of the centurion, a man who did not have the same benefit of religious instruction and upbringing as the disciples, yet still knew in his heart when he was witnessing the power of God. When we hear this, we might ask ourselves, "Would Jesus be amazed at my faith?" If we think the answer is no, this is no reason to give up. Rather, we should double our efforts to follow Jesus in faith rather than allowing ourselves to grow complacent. But sometimes

Old Church Window, Hope Helmer, @hopehelmer.

we are so full of uncertainty we feel that's impossible. Doubts crowd our minds like shadows stretching over sunny, rolling hills before a storm and we feel weak. In these times we might understandably feel unable to meditate on our death, or to remember Jesus' coming at the end of time, or to think about anything of consequence in general.

Meditating on the Last Things, death especially, can lead us to feel weak and fearful, and this can immobilize us—but only if we forget that our faith is not in ourselves but in Jesus. Life will be full of seasons when we feel more doubtful and scared than full of faith. Liturgical seasons like Advent are made for these human rhythms of life: the ups and downs, the valleys and peaks. During these next weeks of Advent, Jesus wants to call us out of the dark valley of fear to remember his incredible love for us, an undying love that led him from the manger to death on a Cross—for love of us. Jesus is the One who is with us and the One in whom we have faith. Faith is not the state of being without any doubt—that would be impossible for our human nature. Faith, rather, is the gift of grace that allows us to trust in Jesus amid our doubt. When we remember the reality of our bodily death with the gift of faith we have been given in Baptism, the shadows of fear will begin to backtrack across the sky as light breaks upon us.

Examen *(see p. 153)*

(see p. 153)

Song of the Soul That Rejoices in Knowing God Through Faith

I know the fountain well that
   flows and runs,
Though of the night.

I

That everlasting fountain is
  a secret well,
And I know well its home,
Though of the night.

II

Its source I know not, because
  it has none;
But I know that therein all things
   have their source,
Though of the night.

III

I know that nothing can be in
   beauty like it,
And that of it heaven and earth
   do drink,
Though of the night.

IV

I know well it is of depths
   unfathomable,
And that none may ever sound it,
Though of the night.

V

Its brightness never is obscured,
And I know that from it all light
   proceeds,
Though of the night.

VI

I know its streams are so
   abundant,
It waters hell and heaven
   and earth,
Though of the night.

VII

The torrent that from this
   fountain rises

I know well, is so grand and
   so strong,
Though of the night.

VIII

The torrent that from Both
   proceeds,
I know that Neither of them
   It precedes,
Though of the night.

IX

This everlasting fountain lies
   concealed
In the living Bread to give us life,
Though of the night.

X

It calls on every creature to
   be filled
With its waters, but in the darkness,
Though of the night.

XI

This living fount which I desire
I see it in this Bread of life,
Though of the night.

— Saint John of the Cross

Journaling and Prayer

Reflect on a time when doubt overcame you, perhaps to the point of despair. Did you bring your doubts to God? If so, how did he respond? If you did not go to God with your doubts, what kept you from doing so?

SERVARE MODUM, FINEMQUE TUERI,

TURAMQUE SEQUI

First Tuesday of Advent

READINGS: Is 11:1–10 / Ps 72:1–2, 7–8, 12–13, 17 / Lk 10:21–24

At that very moment [Jesus] rejoiced in the holy Spirit and said, "I give you praise, Father, Lord of heaven and earth, for although you have hidden these things from the wise and the learned you have revealed them to the childlike. Yes, Father, such has been your gracious will. All things have been handed over to me by my Father. No one knows who the Son is except the Father, and who the Father is except the Son and anyone to whom the Son wishes to reveal him." Turning to the disciples in private he said, "Blessed are the eyes that see what you see. For I say to you, many prophets and kings desired to see what you see, but did not see it, and to hear what you hear, but did not hear it."

— LUKE 10:21–24

THE MYSTERIES OF OUR faith are revealed to the childlike, not the wise and the learned. Even if we have heard Jesus' words in this regard over and over at Mass and In Scripture, we nevertheless still want to be wise and learned. There's power in knowledge—power in knowing more than others, power in thinking more quickly than others, power in knowing what others do not know, power in appearing more holy than others, power in having what others do not. We seek power over others in

Vanitas Still Life, Jacques de Gheyn II (1621).

23

myriad ways, sometimes hidden ways. We can seek power even by trying to appear humble. We think gaining these tiny increments of power over others—passing, temporary power—is vitally important to our self-esteem and to our lives. But God, who created the heavens and the earth, the brains in our heads and the hearts in our chest cavities, is not impressed by our childish attempts to grab at power.

No power we seize for ourselves in this life will ever compare to God's power. In fact, the power we seek is often the opposite of God's power. God demonstrates his power to us by divesting himself of it and becoming incarnate: "Who, though he was in the form of God, did not regard equality with God something to be grasped. Rather, he emptied himself, taking the form of a slave, coming in human likeness" (Phil 2:6–7). The childlike know this paradoxical power of God because they recognize their smallness before him. They know that real power lies in acknowledging our weakness before God, who protects us and cares for us. The children of God do not seek power outside of God's will and can thus curl up confidently in the hand of their Father and rest. In the care of the Father, we can be humble and unafraid of anything that might come, even death.

Examen *(see p. 153)*

One of the novices, greatly discouraged at the thought of her imperfections, tells us that [Saint Thérèse of Lisieux] spoke to her as follows:

"You make me think of a little child that is learning to stand but does not yet know how to walk. In his desire to reach the top of the stairs to find his mother, he lifts his little foot to climb the first step. It is all in vain, and at each renewed effort he falls. Well, be like that little child. Always keep lifting your foot to climb the ladder of holiness, and do not imagine that you can mount even the first step. All God asks of you is good will. From the top of the ladder he looks lovingly upon you, and soon, touched by your fruitless efforts, he will himself come down, and, taking you in his arms, will carry you to his kingdom never again to leave him. But should you cease to raise your foot, you will be left for long on the earth."

— *Counsels and Reminiscences of Soeur Thérèse, the Little Flower of Jesus*

Journaling and Prayer

Imagine yourself as a child in the hand of God the Father, resting in his love. Close your eyes and remain in this place for at least five minutes. Rest in silence and let God wrap his love around you. Do you trust in God's unconditional love for you? Ask God to increase your trust in his love.

First Wednesday of Advent

READINGS: Is 25:6–10a / Ps 23:1–3a, 3b–4, 5, 6 / Mt 15:29–37

On this mountain the Lord of hosts
    will provide for all peoples
A feast of rich food and choice wines,
    juicy, rich food and pure, choice wines.
On this mountain he will destroy
    the veil that veils all peoples,
The web that is woven over all nations.
    He will destroy death forever.
The Lord God will wipe away
    the tears from all faces;
The reproach of his people he will remove
    from the whole earth; for the Lord has spoken.
    On that day it will be said:
"Indeed, this is our God; we looked to him, and he saved us!
    This is the Lord to whom we looked;
    let us rejoice and be glad that he has saved us!"
For the hand of the Lord will rest on this mountain.

— Isaiah 25:6–10a

Mary the Chalice, Michelle Arnold Paine,
@paine.michelle.

TODAY'S FIRST READING TELLS us of the mountain on which God will destroy death forever. This mountain, Golgotha, is where Jesus destroyed death on the Cross. There he bled for us, died for us. But his dying for us did not begin there—it began in the manger. Many of us like to neatly divide our spiritual meditations between Lent and Advent. We think Lent is for meditation on the passion of Jesus and Advent for meditation on a warm nativity scene. But Jesus' passion is not separate from the manger. Before he was slammed brutally against the wood of the Cross, Jesus was laid against the wood of the manger by his loving Mother. We may compartmentalize these mysteries because we want to compartmentalize the pain in our lives. But the mystery of our salvation is found as much in the manger as it is on Golgotha, the Place of the Skull.

Throughout our lives, we are invited to stay close to Jesus' manger and upon that mountain on which he destroyed death forever. The mystery of Jesus' passion beckons us from beyond time to stand first beside the manger and then beneath the Cross—to watch him defeat death until the end of time. But do we remain with Jesus? Or do we descend that mountain as soon as possible so we can avoid the pain of life and our faith's mysteries by quieting our hearts with empty sentimentality and pleasure, drowning our suffering in passing things, and smothering our longing with superficial happiness? Rather than running away from Christ, let us seek to live this Advent and Christmas like Christ. Let us allow the wood of the manger to lead us to the wood of the Cross.

Examen *(see p. 153)*

When the unhappy children of Eve abandoned the pursuit of things true and salutary, they gave themselves up to the search for fleeting and perishable things. To whom shall we liken this generation, or to what shall we compare them, seeing that they are unable to tear themselves from earthly and carnal consolations, or disentangle their minds from such trammels? They resemble the shipwrecked who are in danger of being overwhelmed by the waters so they seize eagerly whatever they can first grasp, however frail it may be. And if anyone strives to rescue them, they tend to seize and drag that person down with them, so that not infrequently the rescuer joins them in one common destruction.

Thus, the children of the world perish miserably while following after transitory things and neglect cleaving to those things that are solid and enduring so that their souls may be saved. Of truth, not of vanity, it is said: "You shall know the truth, and the truth shall set you free" (Jn 8:32). Do you, therefore, to whom as to little ones God has revealed things hidden from the wise and learned, turn your thoughts with earnestness to what is truly desirable and diligently meditate on this coming of our Lord? Consider who he is that comes, from where he comes, to whom he comes, for what end he comes, when he comes, and in what manner he comes. This is undoubtedly a most useful and praiseworthy consideration, for the Church would not so devoutly celebrate the season of Advent if there were not some great mystery hidden therein.

— Saint Bernard of Clairvaux, *Advent Sermon I*

Journaling and Prayer

Imagine yourself beside the manger. The Infant Jesus is shivering. Pick him up and keep him warm in your arms for a while in silence. Do you remain with Jesus in life's difficulties, or do you seek after him expecting only relief and consolation? How can you spend more time on the mountain with Jesus in your daily life?

First Thursday of Advent

READINGS: Is 26:1–6 / Ps 118:1, 8–9, 19–21, 25–27a / Mt 7:21, 24–27

Jesus said to his disciples: "Not everyone who says to me, 'Lord, Lord,' will enter the Kingdom of heaven, but only the one who does the will of my Father in heaven. . . . Everyone who listens to these words of mine and acts on them will be like a wise man who built his house on rock. The rain fell, the floods came, and the winds blew and buffeted the house. But it did not collapse; it had been set solidly on rock. And everyone who listens to these words of mine but does not act on them will be like a fool who built his house on sand. The rain fell, the floods came, and the winds blew and buffeted the house. And it collapsed and was completely ruined."

— MATTHEW 7:21, 24–27

ON THE SEA OF life, if we do not set out trusting that the Holy Spirit is our wind, the Body of Christ our boat, and God the Father the solid, rocklike foundation of our world, we will begin to sink in sin's bitter storms. In these times of tempest, we will find ourselves capsizing, and in the ensuing struggle, we may have no idea how to right ourselves, let alone move forward. Without trust in God, we become stranded, and as our hearts beat in anxiety and angst, we forget even to call out to God to save us. Nothing moves us, nothing breathes life into us, and nothing gives us

Edith Stein, James Langley, @langley.artgram.

31

confidence to continue ahead. Some of us have experienced the real, existential despair that emerges when we reject our foundation in God and we all have experienced the discouragement that comes with sin, moving away from God.

The foundation we lose when we run from God is real; our entire being is completely dependent on God. As Saint Teresa Benedicta of the Cross (Edith Stein) wrote of God,

> You are the space
> That embraces my being and buries it in yourself.
> Away from you it sinks into the abyss.

We run from our own being when we run from God because he is the source of our being, the One who keeps all the world in existence, from the rolling ocean waters to the drooping sail. Forgetfulness of this reality, and our feeble attempts to escape it, are the consequences of sin and the constant burden of the suffering human. Meditating on the Last Things, especially death, is a welcome, regular blast of wind in our lives that can right our boats and remind us that God is our life and the source of all life. Remembering death lifts our sails and sends us into new waters on a course to heaven. Because when we remember death, we also remember that the foundation of the seas, of the world, and of life itself is God, who created the heavens, the earth, and the very hearts beating within our chests.

Examen *(see p. 153)*

> Your mercy, Lord, helped me. Not my own strength, but your mercy. . . .
> Consider the world to be the sea; the wind is boisterous, and there is a mighty tempest. Each person's particular lust is his tempest. You love God; you walk upon the sea, and under your feet is the swelling of the world. If you love the world, it will swallow you up. It only knows how to devour its lovers, not to carry them. But when your heart is tossed about by lust, in order that you may get the better of your lust, call upon the divinity of Christ. Do you think that the wind is contrary when there's

adversity in this life? When there are wars, when there is tumult, when there is famine, when there is pestilence, when private calamity arrives to us, then the wind is thought to be contrary, then it is thought that God must be called upon. But when the world wears her smile of temporal happiness, it is as if there were no contrary wind. But do not ask upon this matter the tranquil state of the world: ask only your own lust. . . .

Learn then to tread upon the world; remember to trust in Christ. And if your foot has slipped; if you totter, if there are some things that you cannot overcome, if you begin to sink, say, "Lord, I perish, save me." Say, "I perish," that you perish not. For only he can deliver you from the death of the body, he who died in the body for you. Let us turn to the Lord.

— Saint Augustine, *Sermon 26 on the New Testament*

Journaling and Prayer

Close your eyes and imagine yourself sailing on the sea of life. Imagine the kind of boat you are in and feel your speed—both at the highest points in your life and the lowest. Bring what you imagine to Jesus in prayer. Who—or what—do you make the foundation of your life? Where do you go to seek comfort and help when your ship meets storms?

HOMINEM TE ESSE MEMENTO

First Friday of Advent

READINGS: Is 29:17–24 / Ps 27:1, 4, 13–14 / Mt 9:27–31

As Jesus passed on from there, two blind men followed [him], crying out, "Son of David, have pity on us!" When he entered the house, the blind men approached him and Jesus said to them, "Do you believe that I can do this?" "Yes, Lord," they said to him. Then he touched their eyes and said, "Let it be done for you according to your faith." And their eyes were opened. Jesus warned them sternly, "See that no one knows about this." But they went out and spread word of him through all that land.

— MATTHEW 9:27–31

IN TODAY'S GOSPEL JESUS heals two blind men. We too suffer from a kind of blindness, one far more serious than physical blindness: the blindness of the soul in sin. When we sin it is as if we walk from a sunlit backyard into a cellar. Wet darkness descends abruptly and envelops us. All sense of our bodies is lost, our minds feel as if they are suspended in air, and our thoughts race as we grope along the wall, but nothing gives clarity. Sin has cast us far from ourselves and from God. Then as our hands grope the darkness, we find another human form. His hand extends to us and gently touches our eyes. Blinking, our bodies and minds are restored to the light.

Remember You're Just a Man,
Daniela Madriz de Quintana, @daniela.madriz.design.

Jesus' physical healings in Scripture point toward a far deeper heal-ing that humanity experiences through his incarnation, death, and resur-rection. Conversion restores our senses and opens the eyes of our soul. Just as in the Gospel, Christ touches our eyes in these moments. He comes close, so close that we can feel his breath on our faces. The God-man rests his fingers on our closed eyelids, and light suddenly pierces the darkness. Small turns toward Christ are all we need to find his hands outstretched to us, ready to flood our souls with light. We don't realize how dark our lives can be until we make this turn. When we meditate on our death, a consequence of sin, we enter into darkness, yes, but we enter to meet Christ our Light within it. Meditation on death is a turning toward the light of Christ, not the darkness of death, because he will be on the other side of death. We remember death to remember Christ, and his light pierces the darkness.

Examen *(see p. 153)*

My dear Redeemer, how I have been so blind as to abandon you—who are infinite goodness, and the fountain of all consolation—for the miserable and momentary gratifications of the senses? I am astonished at my blind-ness, but I am still more astonished at your mercy, which has so bounti-fully borne with me. I thank you for making me aware now of my folly, and of my obligation to love you. I love you, O my Jesus, with my whole soul, but I desire to love you with greater fervor. Increase my desire and my love. Enamor my soul of you, who are infinitely lovable; of you, who have left nothing undone to gain my love; of you, who so ardently desire my love. "If you will it, you can make me clean" (see Mt 8:2).

Ah, my dear Redeemer, purify my heart from all impure affections, which hinder me from loving you as I would wish! It is not in my power to inflame my whole heart with the love of you, and to make it love nothing but you. This requires the power of your grace, which can do all things. Detach me from every creature, banish from my soul every affection which is not for you, make me all yours. . . . I resolve to consecrate all the days of my life to your holy love; but it is only your grace that can make me fulfill this resolution. Grant me, O Lord, this grace for the sake of the Blood which you shed for me with so much pain and so much love. Let it be the glory of your power to make my heart, which was once full of earthly affections, now become all flames of love for you, O infinite Good. O Mother of Fair Love, O Mary, by your prayers, make my whole soul burn, as yours did, with the charity of God.

— Saint Alphonsus Liguori, *Preparation for Death*

Journaling and Prayer

Close your eyes and imagine Jesus drawing near to heal you as he did the two blind men. What does Jesus want to heal in you? What do you ask him to heal in you? What is his response? Sit in this meditation for some time. How has the light of conversion pierced your life? What did it show you about God's love?

REMEMBER YOUR DEATH

First Saturday of Advent

READINGS: Is 30:19–21, 23–26 / Ps 147:1–2, 3–4, 5–6 / Mt 9:35–10:1, 5a, 6–8

Jesus went around to all the towns and villages, teaching in their synagogues, proclaiming the gospel of the kingdom, and curing every disease and illness. At the sight of the crowds, his heart was moved with pity for them because they were troubled and abandoned, like sheep without a shepherd. Then he said to his disciples, "The harvest is abundant but the laborers are few; so ask the master of the harvest to send out laborers for his harvest."

— MATTHEW 9:35–38

JESUS' HEART IS MOVED with pity for the people in today's Gospel, and it also moves with pity for us. But we are not always open to his pity; we do not like to be in need of it. Instead, we want to be self-sufficient and deserving of praise, even God's praise. But meditation on death helps us to realize that we are in fact incredibly pitiable and helpless. Whether we are mindful of it or not, death creeps toward us every day, not even bothering to hide the sound of its footsteps. There's nothing we can do to muffle its approach or effects. We are powerless over death—O inevitable death! We are death-bound sinners in need of grace. This might

Remember Your Death,
Cory and Marie Heimann, @LikableArt @fawnlyprints.

sound too negative, too much like "worm theology" that denigrates the human person. But this is not about wallowing in shame or self-pity. Rather, this is simple fact. In order to more fully accept God's love and to truly live out of our dignity as created in the image of God, we must first acknowledge before him that we are sinful and helpless.

Many people shudder at the thought of meditating on the Last Things because deep down we don't want to admit that we are pitiable because of sin. But when we give up these uncomfortable aspects of our faith, we also give up the paradoxical comfort found in contemplating them. Accepting that we are pitiable is the first step to accepting the grace that God gives us to save us from ourselves. The compassionate movement of Jesus' Sacred Heart wraps us in the power of his Blood and allows us to rest in the warmth of God's protection and love. This can bring us great relief from our suffering. When we recognize our smallness, we also begin to understand more fully how God's love surrounds us in our weakness. His overwhelming love for helpless humanity, the movement of salvation, culminates in the Son of God's astounding descent in the Incarnation that we contemplate in this silent season.

Examen *(see p. 153)*

(see p. 153)

Saint Mechtilde to Jesus: "O sweetest Jesus, if it is so pleasing to you that humanity should trust in you, tell me, I pray, what should I believe about your ineffable goodness?"

Our Lord replied: "You must believe with a firm hope that after your death I will receive you as a father receives his well-beloved child, that I will share all that I have with you and will give you part of myself. Further, I will receive you as a friend receives his dearest friend and I will show you a greater love than friend ever received from friend. I will also receive you as a spouse receiving his new bride whom he loves intensely, with so much delight and sweetness. No spouse ever multiplied for his bride so much tenderness as I will lavish on you, filling you with joy and inebriating you with a torrent of happiness from my divinity."

Saint Mechtilde replied: "What will you give to those who trust in these promises?"

Our Lord answered: "I will give them a thankful heart, with which they will receive my gifts gratefully; I will give them a loving heart, with which they will love me faithfully; and lastly I will give them hearts to praise me as the heavenly choirs praise me, loving and blessing me always."

— Saint Mechtilde, *The Book of Special Grace*

Journaling and Prayer

Imagine you are one of the people in today's Gospel, and Jesus is beholding you with pity and love. What is your reaction? Observe this reaction for some time in silence and then talk about it with Jesus. In what ways do you resist God's love for you? Does intimacy with God frighten you? What about God's love do you resist?

Second Week of Advent

JUDGMENT

Advent is tailor-made for meditation on judgment. As we've seen, the word "advent," which means "arrival," applies both to Jesus' coming at our particular judgment at the moment of our deaths and the general judgment at the end of the world. Therefore, when we meditate on judgment, we are considering these two arrivals of Jesus that await us. The liturgical readings for Advent, especially in the first weeks, also focus us on this theme. The time before Christmas in the modern world, on the other hand, is rarely conducive to quiet spiritual preparation for judgment.

In the hubbub of holiday shopping, work parties, and card writing, it can be a struggle to focus on Advent's penitential emphasis and meditate on something as uncomfortable and abstract as the idea of being judged by God. Meditating on our judgment, after all, involves a penitential delay of the comfort that can come with all that surrounds the Christmas season. Indeed, the thought of God's judgment should not bring us the kind of comfort that twinkling lights and the smell of pine boughs bring us at Christmastime. After all, if we are comfortable with the thought of being judged by God, perhaps we are forgetting both our own weakness and God's transcendence. As Saint Augustine once wrote, "If you understood him, it would not be God."

Catholicism does not give us effortlessly understandable, easily categorized, and generally unintimidating soothing, simplistic truths. As Pope Emeritus Benedict XVI once put it, "Those who desire comforts have dialed the wrong number." At times, this difficult reality can tempt us to reject the dogmas and doctrines that make us uncomfortable and settle for a simplistic relationship with our faith. But we are called to enter the mysteriousness of the paradoxical truths of our faith, even the parts of it—such as judgment—that challenge or unsettle us. At the same time, penitential practices like meditation on the Last Things during Advent are not meant to make us miserable! Meditating on our judgment may stir up uncomfortable feelings and force us to face difficult realities, but God's judgment is not like imperfect human judgments. Instead, the particular and general judgments are about God's truth; in judgment he reveals to us the full truth about ourselves by looking upon us with love.

When we take the time to consider God's look of love upon us in our judgment and the many reasons why we need a Savior, we can more fully experience the joy of Christmas. Meditation on our judgment in light of the Incarnation of the Son of God helps us to reflect on the difference the birth of Christ makes in our judgment at the end of our lives. Meditation on judgment in this way, rather than filling us with fear, can lead us to experience a deep gratitude for the God who reached into the depths of sin, the depths of darkness, and the depths of hell and pulled us out. Now that's a comforting truth of our faith.

> The New Testament speaks of judgment primarily in its aspect of the final encounter with Christ in his second coming, but also repeatedly affirms that each will be rewarded immediately after death in accordance with his works and faith. The parable of the poor man Lazarus and the words of Christ on the Cross to the good thief, as well as other New Testament texts speak of a final destiny of the soul—a destiny which can be different for some than for others.
>
> Each man receives his eternal retribution in his immortal soul at the very moment of his death, in a particular judgment that refers his life to Christ: either entrance into the blessedness of heaven—through a purification or immediately—or immediate and everlasting damnation.
>
> At the evening of life, we shall be judged on our love . . . [Saint John of the Cross, *Dichos* 64].
>
> The Last Judgment will come when Christ returns in glory. Only the Father knows the day and the hour; only he determines the moment of its coming. Then through his Son Jesus Christ he will pronounce the final word on all history. We shall know the ultimate meaning of the whole work of creation and of the entire economy of salvation and understand the marvelous ways by which his Providence led everything toward its final end. The Last Judgment will reveal that God's justice triumphs over all the injustices committed by his creatures and that God's love is stronger than death.

The message of the Last Judgment calls men to conversion while God is still giving them "the acceptable time . . . the day of salvation" [2 Cor 6:2]. It inspires a holy fear of God and commits them to the justice of the Kingdom of God. It proclaims the "blessed hope" of the Lord's return, when he will come "to be glorified in his saints, and to be marveled at in all who have believed" [Ti 2:13; 2 Thes 1:10].

— *Catechism of the Catholic Church* (nos. 1021–1022, 1040–1041)

The Final Battle, Chris Lewis, @barituscatholic.

Second Sunday of Advent

YEAR A: Is 11:1–10 / Ps 72:1–2, 7–8, 12–13, 17 / Rom 15:4–9 / Mt 3:1–12
YEAR B: Is 40:1–5, 9–11 / Ps 85:9ab, 10, 11–12, 13–14 / 2 Pt 3:8–14 / Mk 1:1–8
YEAR C: Bar 5:1–9 / Ps 126:1–2a, 2b–3, 4–5, 6 / Phil 1:4–6, 8–11 / Lk 3:1–6

John wore clothing made of camel's hair and had a leather belt around his waist. His food was locusts and wild honey.

— MATTHEW 3:4

People of the whole Judean countryside and all the inhabitants of Jerusalem were going out to him and were being baptized by him in the Jordan River as they acknowledged their sins.

— MARK 1:5

He went throughout [the] whole region of the Jordan, proclaiming a baptism of repentance for the forgiveness of sins, as it is written in the book of the words of the prophet Isaiah:

"A voice of one crying out in the desert:
'Prepare the way of the Lord,
make straight his paths.'"

— LUKE 3:3–4

Salome with the Head of John the Baptist,
Jan Adam Kruseman (ca. 1861).

THIS SUNDAY'S GOSPELS GIVE us a picture of the person of John the Baptist. He was a man of razor-sharp focus with no time for anything but God. The details of his austere, disciplined, and dedicated desert life might seem unattainable and unrelatable to us. Yet if we pray with this mysterious man of the Scriptures, we need not feel discomfort in his presence or put off by his way of life. Instead we can feel inspired. If we take the time to consider John the Baptist's dazzling life and to ask for his intercession from heaven, the thought of his life led only for God can pour fuel on the small flicker of fervor in our souls. Then we will begin to want, or at least want to want, God as much as he did.

When we remember our judgment, John the Baptist's life can remind us of the razor-sharp focus asked of us, and made accessible to us, as Christians. John baptized people in water as a sign of repentance for their sins, but we have been baptized in the Holy Spirit, who wipes away our original sin and gives us the grace to avoid sin. The same grace that impelled John the Baptist to live completely for God up until the moment he was beheaded dwells in our hearts through Baptism. So if we feel lazy presumption at the thought of our judgment, remembering the focused holiness of John the Baptist can motivate us to ask God to convert our hearts before we are judged by God. And if we feel afraid at the thought of our death and judgment, his bold trust in God also can be an inspiration to us. Like John the Baptist, we are made to be centered in the God who dwells in us through our Baptism. The more we remember that death and judgment await us, the more our hearts will catch fire in the light of the Holy Spirit that dwells in us, and the more we will be impelled to live for heaven now, focused on the loving God who awaits us.

Examen *(see p. 153)*

In imitation of Saint John the Baptist, prepare your heart for all that the Holy Spirit wishes to work in you for his own glory and for the benefit of souls. As far as depends upon you, love solitude and withdraw your soul from the confusion of created things. . . . Seek always your own sanctification and the edification of your neighbor, so that in your outward conversation and communication, the zeal of your spirit may shine forth.

   The exalted virtues . . . resplendent in the lives of other saints, should serve you as a spur and as an example. Seek, like a busy bee, to build up the sweet honeycomb of sanctity and innocence so much desired in you by my divine Son. Distinguish well between the labors of the bee and of the spider: the one converts her nourishment into sweetness useful for the living and the dead, while the other changes it into snare and venom. Gather the flowers of virtue from the saints in the garden of the Church, as far as your weak endeavors with the aid of grace will permit. Imitate the saints eagerly and encourage others to do so by your eloquence, thus drawing blessings upon the living and the dead while you anxiously fly from the harm and damage of sinful deeds.

— Venerable Mary of Jesus of Ágreda, *Mystical City of God*

Journaling and Prayer

   Imagine you have gone out to the desert, to the Jordan River, to see John the Baptist preach. Approach him and ask him to baptize you as a sign of your repentance. After he baptizes you, stay a while in his presence. Ask him questions. What does he say to you in words, gestures, or deeds? How does God invite you into the desert to live as John the Baptist lived? What might God be asking of you right now that seems very hard?

Second Monday of Advent

READINGS: Is 35:1–10 / Ps 85:9ab, 10, 11–12, 13–14 / Lk 5:17–26

One day as Jesus was teaching, Pharisees and teachers of the law were sitting there who had come from every village of Galilee and Judea and Jerusalem, and the power of the Lord was with him for healing. And some men brought on a stretcher a man who was paralyzed; they were trying to bring him in and set [him] in his presence. But not finding a way to bring him in because of the crowd, they went up on the roof and lowered him on the stretcher through the tiles into the middle in front of Jesus. When he saw their faith, he said, "As for you, your sins are forgiven." Then the scribes and Pharisees began to ask themselves, "Who is this who speaks blasphemies? Who but God alone can forgive sins?" Jesus knew their thoughts and said to them in reply, "What are you thinking in your hearts? Which is easier, to say, 'Your sins are forgiven,' or to say, 'Rise and walk'? But that you may know that the Son of Man has authority on earth to forgive sins"—he said to the man who was paralyzed, "I say to you, rise, pick up your stretcher, and go home." He stood up immediately before them, picked up what he had been lying on, and went home, glorifying God. Then astonishment seized them all and they glorified God, and, struck with awe, they said, "We have seen incredible things today."

— LUKE 5:17–26

On the Last Day, Ryan McQuade, @ryanmcq.

MANY ASPECTS OF LIFE can paralyze our hearts. Overwhelming stress, illness, trauma, memories of abuse, the consequences of our own sin or that of others, the death of people we love, or our own impending death can impact us deeply. We all have times in our lives when we are not sure we can hold in our hearts all of this suffering. In these times, the lead of suffering can deaden our limbs. We might feel powerless to move, to seek holiness or friendship, or to feel anything but sorrow. Weighed down by the blurred pain of paralysis, we are helpless, still. Ordinarily, the thought of our death and judgment can shake us from the stupor of suffering and give perspective, but at times even this does not jolt us awake. Yet remembrance of death and judgment is not useless in these situations. While we may feel tempted to abandon spiritual practices when we feel useless, paralyzed, and sinful, Jesus is with us.

In today's Gospel a man is carried by his friends to Jesus and is healed of his paralysis. Perhaps the man was so depressed that he did not desire to be healed, but God found a way to heal him. Sometimes when we meditate on death and judgment, all we can do is ponder our powerlessness and the great powerlessness of humanity without Jesus—and that is enough. We generally like our spiritual practices to help us to visibly improve our lives rather than help us to ponder our weakness. But we can find unexpected joy in acknowledging the depths of our weakness and allowing ourselves to be helped by Jesus. Then, on a day we least expect it, as we ponder our helplessness and wonder if our paralysis will end, we will hear a commanding voice pierce the fog, "Rise!" And we rise—only and fully on the strength of the grace of God.

Examen (see p. 153)

Consider the plight you were in, and what has been done for you. Think too, who did this for you and the kind of love he deserves. Review your need and his goodness and see what thanks on the one hand you give him, and on the other how much you owe to his love. For you were in darkness, on slippery ground, on a slope sheering down to the chaos of hell from which none may return. An enormous weight, like some load of lead hanging from your neck, dragged you lower and lower; a burden too heavy to bear pressed upon you from above. And unseen foes urged you on, in spite of your struggles to get free. Thus were you, without all help, and you did not understand your plight, for thus had you been conceived and born. . . .

O good Christ, O Lord Jesus, without seeking you, nor thinking of you, you shone upon me like a sun, and showed me in what a predicament I was. You threw away the leaden weight that dragged me down. You removed the burden that weighed upon me. You drove away the foes who pursued me and stood against them in my defense. . . . Thus destitute, thus helpless, Jesus, you shone upon me, and showed me the state I was in. . . . For even when as yet I could not know or be aware of it, you taught it to others, who learned on my behalf, and afterward you taught me whenever I sought it of you. The dragging lead, the pressing load, the urging foes—you rid me of them all. For you took away the sin in which I was conceived and born, both the sin and its condemnation, and you have warded off the spiteful fiends from doing violence to my soul. . . . Cling to him, O my soul; cling, cling with insistence. Good Lord, good Lord, cast me not away; I faint with hunger for your love. Revive my soul; let your sweet election satiate it, and your unfailing fondness nourish it, and your divine love fulfill it, and occupy me altogether, and possess and fill me through and through. For you are with the Father and the Holy Spirit, blessed God for ever and ever. Amen.

— Saint Anselm, *Eleventh Meditation*

Journaling and Prayer

Remember a time that you felt helpless and overwhelmed by illness, sorrow, or suffering. Imagine you are the man in today's Gospel. You are lying on a mat and your friends bring you to Jesus. You feel helpless even to ask for help; your friends ask for you. How do you feel in a position of helplessness? Are you angry? Thankful? What do you experience after Jesus heals you?

Second Tuesday of Advent

READINGS: Is 40:1–11 / Ps 96:1–2, 3–10ac, 11–12, 13 / Mt 18:12–14

Jesus said to his disciples: "What is your opinion? If a man has a hundred sheep and one of them goes astray, will he not leave the ninety-nine in the hills and go in search of the stray? And if he finds it, amen, I say to you, he rejoices more over it than over the ninety-nine that did not stray. In just the same way, it is not the will of your heavenly Father that one of these little ones be lost."

— MATTHEW 18:12–14

GOD WANTS US TO be saved and we can trust in his mercy. Meditation on judgment should always begin by remembering what Jesus tells us in today's Gospel: it is not the will of our heavenly Father that we be lost. God does not want even one of us, his little ones, to be lost. But if we know ourselves, our weaknesses, and the extent to which we need God's help to avoid sin, we know we can neither despair of God's mercy nor carelessly presume it. So we should prepare for judgment with both trust and caution, without traces of either desperate anxiety or haughty arrogance. As Saint Paul exhorts in his letter to the Philippians, "Work out your salvation with fear and trembling" (2:12).

Memento Mori Still Life, Cory Mendenhall, @ForDustThouArt.

Trust and fear: the tension of holding these paradoxical attitudes together is the proper stance of a human being before God. That we can both fear and trust a loving God may seem impossible to some, but Saint Thomas Aquinas makes a distinction in his *Summa Theologiae* that can help us to see how we can have both fear and trust before God at the same time. Aquinas explains the difference between two types of fear: servile fear is fear of punishment, while filial fear is that fear "whereby a son fears to offend his father or to be separated from him" (ST II–II, q. 19, a. 10). In other words, proper fear of God is fear of displeasing him rather than simply fearing punishment. The only thing we need fear is separation from God. Like an infant unable to feed or clean herself, we are led by filial fear to rest in the Father's arms and trust that all will be well. We do not save ourselves by this gesture, but it's all God needs from us: our small efforts and trust. He does the rest.

Examen *(see p. 153)*

You must not neglect meditation. Meditate particularly on the miseries of this life, that you may not be too much taken up with its pleasures. Meditate, also, much on death, that you may not be attached to this life; and on the shortness of time, that it may prepare you for eternity. But there is too an endless eternity, where we may feel the most bitter regrets for the loss of that time we now trifle with. How good a use we should make of the few moments God gives us here! If we neglect them, we lose an eternity. I sometimes fear your dear heart thinks too much of this world, of which you have not yet tasted the many miseries. Oh, be not careless. You know, dear love, we cannot tell at what moment we may both meet before the awful tribunal; and then, perhaps, you will thank me for reminding you. . . .

Here is the first day of Advent, and we ought to keep in mind, chiefly, the judgment. Never cease praying, my sweet friend, that we may meet one another joyfully in that day of terrors. When we think of the eternity which follows, we may well tremble . . . [but] our dearest Lord will protect you. May he reunite us all, if it is his holy will, in this world; and if not here, in heaven. Ah, all our endeavors, then, should be to reach that happy abode. The road through life is strewed with thorns—there are many parting tears and many sorrows. We can hardly perceive them fully till youth is past; but we will pray for one another, and walk on resolutely, loving one another, serving our blessed Lord together so that we may love him together for eternity.

— Saint Elizabeth Ann Seton, *Letter (1811)*

Journaling and Prayer

Recall a time you felt lost and Jesus saved you, whether through the help of others or through a grace experienced in prayer. Does this memory lead you to gratitude for God's help and mercy? Or do you think you "deserve" heaven or that the gift of salvation is inevitable? Do you take credit for your virtue or do you see it as a gift from God? Are you grateful to Jesus for saving you? Spend some time in grateful prayer.

IT IS IN DYING THAT WE ARE BORN TO ETERNAL LIFE

Second Wednesday of Advent

READINGS: Is 40:25–31 / Ps 103:1–2, 3–4, 8–10 / Mt 11:28–30

Jesus said to the crowds: "Come to me, all you who labor and are burdened, and I will give you rest. Take my yoke upon you and learn from me, for I am meek and humble of heart; and you will find rest for yourselves. For my yoke is easy, and my burden light."

— MATTHEW 11:28–30

OUT OF LOVE FOR us, Jesus asks us to carry his yoke in today's Gospel. Carrying Jesus' yoke involves striving to live virtuously, practicing our faith with fervor, and living for God with our eyes fixed on eternal life. Despite Jesus' assurance that his yoke is easy and light, at times all these things can seem far too difficult. Indeed we even might feel angry or bitter at the idea of carrying such a yoke. Why should we have to take upon ourselves this unpleasant burden? We also might be repulsed at the idea of having to carry a yoke like a farm animal, let alone a really difficult one. We want to live in freedom without a yoke! So we try throwing it off and galloping away to dry pastures of pleasure and forgetfulness. Little do we know that the things with which we try to replace Jesus' yoke will become another yoke—a yoke of steel and burning, searing pain, the far heavier yoke of sin.

Little Deaths, Joe Kim, @palcampaign.

The yoke Jesus asks us to carry is the yoke of the Cross (see Lk 9:23). Regularly meditating on the Last Things involves carrying this cross, so it can feel arduous, but only if we forget that this meditation is an invitation to grow closer to Jesus. Carrying Jesus' yoke with him is difficult, yes, but it's far less burdensome than the yoke of sin. When we embrace the yoke of Jesus by dying to ourselves, we receive a peace that only Jesus can give (see Jn 14:27). Always by our side, Jesus carries our cross with us as we make our way toward Golgotha, the Place of the Skull. He never expects us to carry our cross alone, and this makes all the difference. When we become fearful at the thought of the death and judgment that await us at the end of our lives, Jesus puts his hand on our shoulders and says, "Trust in me. There's more." Just as there was more than carrying the cross to death for Jesus, there will be more for us also, in this life and in the next.

Examen *(see p. 153)*

[In our time] you can find ways of thinking and living that are the complete opposite of Christian asceticism. People often have a false notion of Christian asceticism, a pagan notion of physical activity and material satisfaction that is to the detriment of the higher values of the interior life and the much nobler and more intense happiness it offers us. These notions creep into young people's thinking and give rise to a pagan mentality that seems like a wonderful glorification of life but that, in reality, when it does not lead to ruin and death, tarnishes life. . . . This mentality says that spirituality is a pretense; it rejects life, makes people gloomy, damages their health, is against nature, etc.

[In reality,] the practice of the interior life imposes sacrifices that, little by little, become pleasant: "For my yoke is easy, and my burden is light," said the Divine Teacher. This holy yoke keeps us free of worldly concerns; in many cases it eliminates life's most weighty sufferings (the anguish of doubt, remorse, distress), it alleviates suffering . . . [the spiritual life] not only allows but intensifies all lawful enjoyment (such as the contemplation of nature, the enjoyment of the sciences, the profound and rapturous delight of art, the savoring of the earth's most variegated gifts and fruits, homely joys, the delight that comes from healthy enjoyment, and so on); that itself extracts a whole treasury of quite pure and inexpressible delights, a fruit of service to God, an outcome of God's possession. . . . Christian perfection is to live in Jesus Christ, and our incorporation in him is the basis and motive of imitation of Jesus Christ, of our spiritual progression toward him and of our life of union with him.

— Blessed James Alberione

Journaling and Prayer

Consider a time when you were burdened by work, family trouble, or personal issues. Take some time in prayer to share your burdens, past and present, with Jesus. Imagine him lifting the load from your shoulders and carrying it with you. Do your burdens lead you to despair or hope? What helps you to be hopeful when you carry your burdens? Do you tend to share your burdens with Jesus? Why or why not?

O DEATH
WHERE IS
Y   OUR
VICTORY

First Epistle to
the Corinthians
15:55-57

Second Thursday of Advent

READINGS: Is 41:13–20 / Ps 145:1–9, 10–11, 12–13ab / Mt 11:11–15

Jesus said to the crowds: "Amen, I say to you, among those born of women there has been none greater than John the Baptist; yet the least in the Kingdom of heaven is greater than he. From the days of John the Baptist until now, the Kingdom of heaven suffers violence, and the violent are taking it by force. All the prophets and the law prophesied up to the time of John. And if you are willing to accept it, he is Elijah, the one who is to come. Whoever has ears ought to hear."

— MATTHEW 11:11–15

JESUS TELLS THE CROWDS in today's Gospel, "Whoever has ears ought to hear." The people must have been confused when they heard this. Some must have thought, "What exactly does he mean? How can I make sure I have the ears to hear?" Sober, humble people in touch with their weakness realize they often are hard of hearing when it comes to listening to God's voice in their lives. Sin muffles God's invitations. The world screams, God whispers. Even if we regularly take time to pray, we can still struggle to hear God's whispers in the dark silence of prayer. But we especially find it difficult if we are not giving prayer the proper emphasis. Taking time to pray does not necessarily mean that hearing God will suddenly become easy, but if we regularly give God our ears in prayer, we can be sure he will speak.

We often take time to listen carefully for God's voice in the din at pivotal moments, times of great stress, or before forks in the road. In these times when the inner ears of our hearts listen more intently, God can speak with the clarity of crisp mountain air. God knows when we need to hear something clearly, and then every cell in our bodies will hear his voice. With our ears attuned to God's grace, we can then move forward in the direction of his voice with more confidence. Even if we suddenly stop hearing his voice again, we are surer he is still calling. God gives us these moments to show us that when we set aside time in our lives to hear his voice, he will give us the clarity we need. God always gives us the grace and just enough clarity to continue walking toward our death, our judgment, and heaven—toward him—with our heads held high.

Examen *(see p. 153)*

(see p. 153)

This is my God, the Lord of all, who alone stretched out the heaven, and established the breadth of the earth under it; who stirs the deep recesses of the sea and makes its waves roar; who rules its power and stills the tumult of its waves; who founded the earth upon the waters and gave a spirit to nourish it; whose breath gives light to the whole; who, if he withdraw his breath, the whole will utterly fail. By him you speak . . . his breath you breathe, yet him you know not. And this is your condition, because of the blindness of your soul, and the hardness of your heart. But if you will, you may be healed.

Entrust yourself to the Physician, and he will couch the eyes of your soul and of your heart. Who is the Physician? God, who heals and makes alive through his word and wisdom. God by his own word and wisdom made all things; for by his word were the heavens made, and all the host of them by the breath of his mouth. Most excellent is his wisdom. By his wisdom God founded the earth; and by knowledge he prepared the heavens; and by understanding were the fountains of the great deep broken up, and the clouds poured out their dew.

If you perceive these things, O man, living chastely, and holily, and righteously, you can see God. But before all let faith and the fear of God have rule in your heart, and then shall you understand these things. When you shall have put off the mortal, and put on incorruption, then shall you see God worthily. For God will raise your flesh immortal with your soul; and then, having become immortal, you shall see the Immortal, if now you believe in him; and then you shall know that you have spoken unjustly against him. . . . For he who gave the mouth for speech, and formed the ear to hear, and made the eye to see, will examine all things, and will judge righteous judgment, rendering merited awards to each. To those who by patient continuance in doing good seek immortality [see Rom 2:7], he will give life everlasting, joy, peace, rest, and abundance of good things, which neither has eye seen, nor ear heard, nor has it entered into our hearts to conceive.

— Saint Theophilus of Antioch, *Apology to Autolycus*

Journaling and Prayer

Sit in prayer with your eyes closed and imagine your ears opening wide. Tell God that you are listening and want to hear anything he has to tell you. Remain in silence for at least several minutes. As you end your time of prayer, be confident that God spoke to you in the silence even if you cannot articulate what he said. How can you listen to God in silence more, especially this Advent?

Second Friday of Advent

READINGS: Is 48:17–19 / Ps 1:1–2, 3, 4–6 / Mt 11:16–19

Jesus said to the crowds: "To what shall I compare this generation? It is like children who sit in marketplaces and call to one another, 'We played the flute for you, but you did not dance, we sang a dirge but you did not mourn.' For John came neither eating nor drinking, and they said, 'He is possessed by a demon.' The Son of Man came eating and drinking and they said, 'Look, he is a glutton and a drunkard, a friend of tax collectors and sinners.' But wisdom is vindicated by her works."

— MATTHEW 11:16–19

IN TODAY'S GOSPEL JESUS describes people in a state of perpetual dissatisfaction. Faced with the piety of John the Baptist, these people criticized his austerity. Then when Jesus came and joined in celebrations, laughing and drinking wine, the same people judged him for enjoying life. One can deduce from these criticisms that the people making them perhaps enjoyed criticizing others, whether there was truth to their words or not. Of course, when we read about situations like this, most of us think we would not have been among the people who criticized Jesus. We tell ourselves that were we alive in his day, we never

Memento Mori Window, Cory Mendenhall, @ForDustThouArt.

69

would have opposed him. But what makes us so sure? If we indulge in criticism and judgment of others regularly in our daily life, it's possible we would have criticized even the Son of God.

What causes the bitter poison of grumbling and a critical spirit? Most often, it's the result of pride. Perpetual dissatisfaction with the reality of life could be a sign of a prideful, self-satisfied soul. In this state, even the thought of death, judgment, and hell may not deter us—we might mistakenly think we can conquer even those things. The spirit of criticism douses the fervent heart in cool self-sufficiency and arrogance. Yet the reality is that while we all have sinned and are thus deserving of criticism, God chose to save us. Rather than sitting back and folding his arms in haughty, critical detachment, God stooped down to save us. Godly criticism, unlike the hostile criticism of pride, is always joined with Christlike mercy. Godly criticism is also deeply humble, fully realizing that at our own judgment God's critique of our lives would not be in our favor were it not for Jesus Christ. While none of us are without sin or fault, we can be thankful that God's judgment will be far more just and merciful than our own.

Examen *(see p. 153)*

Think of nothing but your salvation, care for nothing but the things of God. Make friends for yourself now, by honoring God's saints and imitating their actions. Then when your life here is over, they will welcome you into everlasting dwellings. Remain a pilgrim and a stranger upon earth, one for whom this world's affairs hold no interest (cf. 1 Pt 2:11). Keep your heart free and raised toward God because you have no lasting home here (cf. Heb 13:14). . . .

In all things look to your end and how you will stand before a severe Judge from whom nothing is hidden, who takes no bribes, nor receives excuses, but will judge that which is just (cf. Deut 1:16). Oh, miserable and foolish sinner, how will you answer God, who knows all your sins (cf. Job 31:14)? . . . Why not prepare yourself for the Day of Judgment when no one can be excused or defended by another? On that day everyone will have enough to do to answer for himself. . . . Truly we deceive ourselves by the inordinate love we have for our flesh. . . .

Take care now and repent for your sins, that on the Day of Judgment you may be secure with the blessed. "Then the just will stand confidently before those who have afflicted and oppressed them" (Wis 5:1). . . . Surely you cannot have both joys—your pleasure in this world and afterward to reign with Christ. If up to now your life has been filled with honors and pleasures, what was the purpose if you die today? All, then, is vanity, except to love God and serve God alone. For one who wholeheartedly loves God fears neither death, nor punishment, nor judgment, nor hell. Perfect love has direct access to God. But he who is still delighted with sin should certainly fear death and judgment.

— Thomas à Kempis, *Imitation of Christ*

Journaling and Prayer

Imagine yourself among the critics of Jesus in his day. What do you think about him? What about him irritates you? Voice the thought to Jesus and see what he says and how he responds. How is God calling you to be less judgmental of others? How could you respond to criticism more humbly?

Paris
Mars 1915

La véritable grandeur d'une
nation se mesure au bien qu'elle fait.
Merci à nos généreux
amis les États Unis
d'Amérique
Sanbès

Second Saturday of Advent

READINGS: Sir 48:1–4, 9–11 / Ps 80:2ac–3b, 15–16, 18–19 / Mt 17:9a, 10–13

As they were coming down from the mountain, the disciples asked Jesus, "Why do the scribes say that Elijah must come first?" He said in reply, "Elijah will indeed come and restore all things; but I tell you that Elijah has already come, and they did not recognize him but did to him whatever they pleased. So also will the Son of Man suffer at their hands." Then the disciples understood that he was speaking to them of John the Baptist.

— MATTHEW 17:9A, 10–13

JESUS TELLS US IN today's Gospel that John the Baptist was not recognized by the people as Elijah. John spoke fiery words of truth that singed the air before him, and still he was not recognized for who he was. What mattered, however, was not whether other people recognized John the Baptist for who he was, but that God did. On the day of our judgment, the opinion of others will neither count for nor against us. At the end of our lives, we will stand before God in the truth of who we are. Hopefully, like John the Baptist, we will have tried our best to do God's will and live in truth. This is what ultimately matters, even if in the eyes of the world we are failures in all other areas of our lives.

Head of John the Baptist, Léon-Daniel Saubès (1915).

Of course, no matter how well we live, our own efforts without God's grace are never enough to open the gates of heaven. But if we accept God's grace to live in truth now, on the day of judgment we can be sure that God's mercy will prevail. To examine how we live in truth, we can ask ourselves whether concerns about personal cost or losing people's admiration lead us to cloak our words in cowardice, pride, defensiveness, indirectness, cruelty, or artifice. In other words, does our "yes mean yes and our no mean no" (see Mt 5:37)? God wants us to smash our facades of insincere kindness, excessive anger, false humility, and sentimental, showy piety in our lives. No matter the consequences to our social life, our wallet, or our résumés, our faith calls us to live in truth now so that we may be prepared to stand before God in truth at our judgment. Living in truth rarely brings us admiration or worldly success, but it does bring freedom both now and at our judgment.

Examen *(see p. 153)*

Religion has (as it were) its very life in what are paradoxes and contradictions in the eye of reason. It is a seeming inconsistency how we can pray for Christ's coming, yet wish time to "work out our salvation," and "make our calling and election sure." It was a seeming contradiction . . . how the apostles feared, yet rejoiced after his resurrection. And so it is a paradox how the Christian should in all things be sorrowful yet always rejoicing, and dying yet living, and having nothing yet possessing all things. Such seeming contradictions arise from the want of depth in our minds to master the whole truth. We have not eyes keen enough to follow out the lines of God's providence and will, which meet at length, though at first sight they seem parallel. . . .

You must tremble, and yet pray for [the future coming of Christ]. We have all of us experienced enough even of this life to know that the same seasons are often most joyful and also most painful. Instances of this must suggest themselves to all. . . . Consider the loss of friends, and say whether joy and grief, triumph and humiliation, are not strangely mingled, yet both really preserved. The joy does not change the grief, nor the grief the joy, into some third feeling; they are incommunicable with each other, both remain, both affect us. Or consider the mingled feelings with which a son obtains forgiveness of a father—the soothing thought that all displeasure is at an end, the veneration, the love, and all the indescribable emotions, most pleasurable, which cannot be put into words—yet his bitterness against himself. Such is the temper in which we desire to come to the Lord's table; such in which we must pray for his coming; such in which his elect will stand before him when he comes.

[And] in that solemn hour we shall have, if we be his, the inward support of his Spirit too, carrying us on toward him, and "witnessing with our spirits that we are the children of God." God is mysteriously threefold; and while he remains in the highest heaven, he comes to judge the world—and while he judges the world, he is in us also, bearing us up and going forth in us to meet himself.

— Saint John Henry Newman, *Shrinking from Christ's Coming*

Journaling and Prayer

Imagine yourself in John the Baptist's presence. You are sitting side by side in the desert while he takes a break from baptizing. What does it feel like to sit in the presence of someone who lives so radically in the truth? Are you afraid? Inspired? Both? Converse with John about how you feel. How can the example of this saint inspire you to live more fully in the truth?

THIRD WEEK OF ADVENT

HELL

On the Third Sunday of Advent, Gaudete Sunday, the liturgy allows for brighter, rose-colored vestments. This Sunday receives its name from the opening antiphon for Mass, "Rejoice in the Lord always," or in Latin, *Gaudete in Domino semper* (Phil 4:4). It may seem odd and inappropriate, then, that this week while we ponder the theme of rejoicing in the coming of the Lord, we also contemplate hell. For hell is the torment of unending separation from God, while Advent celebrates God coming near. But it only seems strange and unsuitable to remember hell during Advent if we have forgotten the meaning of the Incarnation. The joy of our faith rests in the paradoxical reality that, while the faithlessness of our sins deserves hell, the Son of God opened the gates of heaven for us. "God proves his love for us in that while we were still sinners Christ died for us" (Rom 5:8). Therefore, the most fitting reaction to this miraculous mystery, to the awe-inspiring promise of our salvation, is joy.

Unsurprisingly, however, most of us don't experience joy when we think of hell and very few people choose to meditate on hell. Instead, understandably, the thought of hell makes many of us feel angry, doubtful, or fearful. Unfortunately, it does not help that the concept of hell has at times been presented harmfully and has sometimes even been used as a method of control. Some Christians deny the existence of hell for this reason. And others find the very concept of hell incompatible with the reality of an all-powerful, loving God. But God predestines no one to go to hell. God wills all to be saved and to come to knowledge of the truth (see 1 Tm 2:4). Those who go to hell, in a sense, choose it for themselves by deliberately spurning God's merciful love.

Given this, some fear of hell is reasonable and pious, but when we hold the tension and paradox of salvation together, heaven and hell on each side, heaven should always win. Evil and good are not equal adversaries. God, who is Goodness itself, is far more powerful than evil, which is the absence of good. Therefore, in our consideration of hell, God's merciful love must be the mighty conqueror above our fear. Indeed, we need never focus on a fear of hell if our focus remains on the love of God. As Saint John Chrysostom once wrote, "Be it our care therefore, beloved, to understand the love of God. A great thing indeed is this; nothing is so beneficial to us, nothing so deeply touches us: nothing is more availing to convince our souls than even the fear of hell itself." Meditation on hell, therefore, should be a practice centered on God's love for us more than anything else.

Mary, our model and guide in the season of Advent, reveals to us the primacy of joy in the mystery of our salvation. In the Litany of Loreto, we refer to Mary as the "Cause of Our Joy" because her "yes" at the moment of the Annunciation marked the beginning, in a sense, of the joy of our salvation. As Mary accompanied her God-child, born in cold and poverty and destined for death on a Cross, she experienced sorrow but also exuded joy. She found joy in these circumstances because she knew the salvation of the whole world was near. Mary's joy and trust in God colored all she considered and meditated on. She knew God was the center of her life and that her eternity would be spent with him. A Marian consideration of hell then is characterized by joyful trust in God's love, not abject fear. Like Mary, our lives need not be dominated by anxiety but rather by a trusting confidence in God who gives us joy. In the dark winter weeks of Advent, we consider hell according to this Marian joy as well as these words of Saint Paul: "I am convinced that neither death, nor life, nor angels, nor principalities, nor present things, nor future things, nor powers, nor height, nor depth, nor any other creature will be able to separate us from the love of God in Christ Jesus our Lord" (Rom 8:38–39).

> We cannot be united with God unless we freely choose to love him. . . . To die in mortal sin without repenting and accepting God's merciful love means remaining separated from him forever by our own free choice. This state of definitive self-exclusion from communion with God and the blessed is called "hell." . . .
>
> The teaching of the Church affirms the existence of hell and its eternity. Immediately after death the souls of those who die in a state of mortal sin descend into hell, where they suffer the punishments of hell, "eternal fire." The chief punishment of hell is eternal separation from God, in whom alone man can possess the life and happiness for which he was created and for which he longs.

The affirmations of Sacred Scripture and the teachings of the Church on the subject of hell are a call to the responsibility incumbent upon man to make use of his freedom in view of his eternal destiny. They are at the same time an urgent call to conversion: "Enter by the narrow gate; for the gate is wide and the way is easy, that leads to destruction, and those who enter by it are many. For the gate is narrow and the way is hard, that leads to life, and those who find it are few" [Mt 7:13–14].

Since we know neither the day nor the hour, we should follow the advice of the Lord and watch constantly so that, when the single course of our earthly life is completed, we may merit to enter with him into the marriage feast and be numbered among the blessed [*Lumen Gentium* 48].

— *Catechism of the Catholic Church* (nos. 1033, 1035–1036)

The Humbling, Jay Parnell, jayparnell.com.

Third Sunday of Advent

Year A: Is 35:1–6a, 10 / Ps 146:6c–7, 8–9a, 9b–10 / Jas 5:7–10 / Mt 11:2–11
Year B: Is 61:1–2a, 10–11 / Lk 1:46–48, 49–50, 53–54 / 1 Thes 5:16–24 /
    Jn 1:6–8, 19–28
Year C: Zep 3:14–18a / Is 12:2–3, 4bcd, 5–6 / Phil 4:4–7 / Lk 3:10–18

Say to the fearful of heart:
    Be strong, do not fear!

— Isaiah 35:4

"My soul proclaims the greatness of the Lord;
    my spirit rejoices in God my savior."

— Luke 1:46–47

Rejoice in the Lord always. I shall say it again: rejoice! Your kindness should be known to all. The Lord is near. Have no anxiety at all, but in everything, by prayer and petition, with thanksgiving, make your requests known to God. Then the peace of God that surpasses all understanding will guard your hearts and minds in Christ Jesus.

— Philippians 4:4–7

In the Scripture passage that sets the tone for this entire week, Saint Paul calls the Philippians to "rejoice in the Lord always." Rejoice in the Lord always! It seems an impossible command. Rejoice? Always? But

La Mort Attend (Death Awaits), Harmony Miller, @hrmndesigns.

Paul is not exhorting us to that hellish "joy" of a false enjoyment of licentious pleasure, self-absorbed pride, and selfishness. Rather, Paul speaks of a joy that's deeper than our human capacities and emotions. It's helpful to remember that Paul wrote this command to the church of Philippi from prison, knowing his death was likely around the corner.

In the same letter in which Paul exhorts the people to rejoice always and to "have no anxiety at all" (Phil 4:6), he also admits that he had experienced anxiety because Epaphroditus, a man who was sent by the people of Philippi to visit Paul, had almost died of an illness (see Phil 2:25–30). Paul writes that he had sent the recovered Epaphroditus back to Philippi so that he "may have less anxiety" (Phil 2:28). But then mere lines later, Paul exhorts the people to have no anxiety at all! What could Paul possibly mean by telling the people to not be anxious when he himself had just admitted to feeling fear and anxiety? The same could be asked about his command to rejoice always. How can Paul tell people to rejoice always when it's obviously impossible on a human level? One brief glance at Paul's letters reveals that he clearly did not rejoice always. Surely, he was not rejoicing when he wrote, "O stupid Galatians!" (Gal 3:1).

Saint Paul knew from experience that we cannot ignore our natural human emotions that arise, sometimes despite ourselves. To ignore or suppress our emotions would be to reject how God made us. But amid Paul's humanity, God was his strength in every circumstance. He knew that God's indwelling grace resided in his soul more deeply than passing emotions. The same is true for us. When we feel overwhelmed by sorrow or evil, we can nevertheless still hold onto joy and in a sense rejoice always—because God is our joy. Through our Baptism, we have access to this deep joy that comes from knowing that God has unlocked the gates of heaven and saved us from hell.

Examen (see p. 153)

Have you suffered dishonor? Look to the glory that through patience is stored for you in heaven. Have you suffered loss? Fix your eyes on the heavenly riches, and on the treasure which you have put by for yourself through good works. Have you suffered exile? Your fatherland is the heavenly Jerusalem. Have you lost a child? You have angels with whom you shall dance about the throne of God and be glad with everlasting joy. Set expected joys over and against present griefs, and thus you will preserve for yourself that calm and quiet of the soul to which the injunction of the Apostle [Paul] calls us.

Let not the brightness of human success fill your soul with immoderate joy; let not grief bring low your soul's high and lofty exaltation through sadness and anguish. You must be trained in the lessons of this life before you can live the calm and quiet life to come. You will achieve this without difficulty, if you keep ever with you the charge to rejoice always. Dismiss the worries of the flesh. Gather together the joys of the soul. Rise above the sensible perception of present things. Fix your mind on the hope of things eternal. Of these the mere thought suffices to fill the soul with gladness, and to plant in our hearts the happiness of angels.

— Saint Basil the Great, Homily IV

Journaling and Prayer

How does Saint Paul's call to rejoice resonate with you? What threatens to cloud your joy and trust in God? How do you feel when you read the passages in Scripture where Jesus speaks of hell? Bring your reactions to mentions of hell over the course of your life to Jesus in prayer. Could you learn to find joy in them?

MEMENTO
MORI

Third Monday of Advent

READINGS: Nm 24:2–7, 15–17a / Ps 25:4–5ab, 6–7bc, 8–9 / Mt 21:23–27

When [Jesus] had come into the temple area, the chief priests and the elders of the people approached him as he was teaching and said, "By what authority are you doing these things? And who gave you this authority?" Jesus said to them in reply, "I shall ask you one question, and if you answer it for me, then I shall tell you by what authority I do these things. Where was John's baptism from? Was it of heavenly or of human origin?" They discussed this among themselves and said, "If we say, 'Of heavenly origin,' he will say to us, 'Then why did you not believe him?' But if we say, 'Of human origin,' we fear the crowd, for they all regard John as a prophet." So they said to Jesus in reply, "We do not know." He himself said to them, "Neither shall I tell you by what authority I do these things."

— MATTHEW 21:23–27

JESUS IS ASKED IN today's Gospel where his authority comes from, but, as is often the case, he does not respond. Jesus sees his questioners' insincerity and skepticism and, in freedom and charity, he remains silent. The fact that the chief priests and elders asked where Jesus' authority came from is not at all wrong in itself. But they fell into error by being disingenuous in their questions to Jesus. Before we jump too quickly to

Memento Mori, Tricia Hope Dugat, @providential_co.

judge the chief priests and elders, it might help to consider that sometimes we ask questions in the same way. In our thoughts and deeds, we
too might bitterly wonder, "Does God really have authority over death? If
hell exists and I could go there, how can it be true that God also loves
me?" Our mistake lies not in asking these questions, but in not bringing
them to God.

If we really are in touch with our thoughts and feelings, we will realize
we sometimes carry within ourselves a skepticism and insincerity similar
to that of the chief priests and elders. We too ask questions about our
faith but are unwilling to wait for or listen to a response. Sometimes we
refuse to listen to Jesus' responses to our questions or we don't even
bother going to him at all. This can be particularly true when it comes to
hell. The Church's teaching on the existence of hell is one that has been
debated, rejected, and scorned by many throughout time. Belief in the
existence of hell requires accepting the sovereignty of God and being
open to the teachings of the tradition, even if they do not always leave
us with a comfortable level of human certainty and solidity.

Taking time for silent prayer creates space where we can ask—and
Jesus answers—our questions. But when we run from our most difficult
questions and from Jesus, we do not find answers when we try to dis-
tract ourselves with pleasure-seeking instead. Even when we are feeling
deeply skeptical, Jesus wants us to bring our doubts and questions to
him in prayer. When we observe signs that we may be avoiding asking
Jesus questions with sincere hearts, we should double our efforts to
turn to him in prayer rather than ignoring or avoiding him. Jesus is always
ready for our questions, even the ones we are frightened to admit we
have. He is listening, bending near to us, and gathering us in his arms. As
long as we bring our questions to him in sincerity and with some degree
of trust, Jesus will respond.

Examen *(see p. 153)*

> In many places Christ speaks obscurely, because he wishes to rouse his
> hearers to ask questions, and to render them more attentive. For what is

said plainly often escapes the hearer but what is obscure renders a person more active and zealous. . . . Let us then cleanse ourselves, let us kindle the light of knowledge, let us not sow among thorns. What the thorns are, you know, though we tell you not; for often you have heard Christ call the cares of this present life, and the deceitfulness of riches, by this name (see Mt 13:22). And with reason. For as thorns are unfruitful, so are these things. As thorns tear those that handle them, so do these passions. As thorns are readily caught by the fire and hateful by the farmer, so too are the things of the world. Just as in thorns wild beasts, snakes, and scorpions hide themselves, so do they in the deceitfulness of riches.

So let us kindle the fire of the Spirit, that we may consume the thorns, and drive away the beasts, and make the field clear for the sower. And after cleansing it, let us water it with the streams of the Spirit, let us plant the fruitful olive, that most kindly of trees, the evergreen, the light-giving, the nutritious, the wholesome. Almsgiving has all these qualities and is a seal on those who possess it. Not even death, when it comes, causes this plant to wither, but ever it stands enlightening the mind, feeding the sinews of the soul, and rendering its strength mightier. And if we constantly possess it, we shall be able with confidence to behold the Bridegroom, and to enter into the bridal chamber; to which may we all attain, through the grace and loving-kindness of our Lord Jesus Christ, with whom to the Father and the Holy Spirit be glory, for ever and ever. Amen.

— Saint John Chrysostom, *Homily 24 on the Gospel of John*

Journaling and Prayer

Imagine yourself eating dinner with Jesus and several of his disciples. You listen intently as the disciples ask him honest, vulnerable questions, and Jesus answers them patiently. Every once in a while, the group breaks out in laughter. Then there is a lull in the conversation. It's your turn to ask Jesus a question. What question will you ask? How does Jesus respond?

Where, O Death, is your victory?
Where, O Death, is your sting?

1 CORINTHIANS 15:55

Third Tuesday of Advent

READINGS: Zep 3:1–2, 9–13 / Ps 34:2–3, 6–7, 17–18, 19–23 / Mt 21:28–32

[Jesus said,] "What is your opinion? A man had two sons. He came to the first and said, 'Son, go out and work in the vineyard today.' He said in reply, 'I will not,' but afterward he changed his mind and went. The man came to the other son and gave the same order. He said in reply, 'Yes, sir,' but did not go. Which of the two did his father's will?" They answered, "The first." Jesus said to them, "Amen, I say to you, tax collectors and prostitutes are entering the kingdom of God before you. When John came to you in the way of righteousness, you did not believe him; but tax collectors and prostitutes did. Yet even when you saw that, you did not later change your minds and believe him."

— MATTHEW 21:28–32

READING TODAY'S GOSPEL PASSAGE may prompt some of us to ask ourselves worriedly, "How does God see my soul?" After all, Jesus is saying that people we might not expect to be in heaven will not only enter it, but enter before others who appear more righteous. Clearly, God's logic of mercy is not our logic. God sees our sin and that of others differently than we do. Jesus' words are a baffling puzzle in a world where we are used to judging by appearances. Most of us, even if we recognize our

Death into New Life, Frica Tighe Campbell, @beaheartdesign.

91

sinfulness to some extent, cannot fathom its depths. Every sin, whether mortal or venial, is evil in that it's a failure to love God, neighbor, and ourselves. Indeed, we may be shocked at the sight of our souls at the moment of judgment, perhaps especially if we think ourselves righteous.

How blind we are to the true evil of sin! Our sin stands in deep contrast to God, who is so pure that we cannot fathom the depth of his purity and the power of his goodness. Before God, our sinfulness is only made more evident. And in the face of this reality that we have no strength to conquer, we can only entrust ourselves to God's goodness, and with his grace, strive against our tendency to sin by receiving the sacraments regularly. However, if we ever think that the heaviness of our sin outweighs God's goodness or that his power cannot obliterate it, we are greatly mistaken. The scales of justice always tip toward the infinite God who stepped on them when the Son of God died on the Cross. Our sin should never lead us to hopelessness. Through his birth, life, death, resurrection, and power, Jesus has defeated the ultimate consequence of sin: death. This truth is completely reliable and constant, unlike our ability to avoid sin. If we trust in Jesus, we will accompany the humble tax collectors and prostitutes who acknowledge their sinfulness before God as they pass joyfully from death into the gates of heaven.

Examen *(see p. 153)*

Of the marvelous wisdom of God in the creation of purgatory and of hell.

As the purified spirit finds no repose but in God, for whom it was created, so the soul in sin can rest nowhere but in hell, which, by reason of its sins, has become its end. Therefore, at that instant in which the soul separates from the body, it goes to its prescribed place, needing no other guide than the nature of the sin itself, if the soul has parted from the body in mortal sin. And if the soul were hindered from obeying that decree (proceeding from the justice of God), it would find itself in a yet deeper hell, for it would be outside of the divine order, in which mercy always finds place and prevents the full infliction of all the pains the soul has merited.

Finding, therefore, no spot more fitting, nor any in which her pains would be so slight, she casts herself into her appointed place.

The same thing is true of purgatory: the soul, leaving the body, and not finding in herself that purity in which she was created, and seeing also the hindrances which prevent her union with God, conscious also that only purgatory can remove them, casts herself quickly and willingly therein. And if she did not find the means ordained for her purification, she would instantly create for herself a hell worse than purgatory, seeing that by reason of this impediment she is hindered from approaching her end, which is God; and this is so great an ill that in comparison with it the soul esteems purgatory as nothing. True it is, as I have said, like hell; and yet, in comparison with the loss of God it is as nothing.

— Saint Catherine of Genoa, *Treatise on Purgatory*

Journaling and Prayer

Imagine you are in purgatory waiting to enter heaven. Who waits with you? Are you surprised you have to wait? Rest in this imaginative prayer for a time. Ask Jesus to show you how prepared you are for heaven and end your prayer by asking him to prepare your soul to meet him.

Third Wednesday of Advent

READINGS: Is 45:6c–8, 18, 21c–25 / Ps 85:9ab–10, 11–12, 13–14 / Lk 7:18b–23

John summoned two of his disciples and sent them to the Lord to ask, "Are you the one who is to come, or should we look for another?" When the men came to him, they said, "John the Baptist has sent us to you to ask, 'Are you the one who is to come, or should we look for another?'" At that time he cured many of their diseases, sufferings, and evil spirits; he also granted sight to many who were blind. And he said to them in reply, "Go and tell John what you have seen and heard: the blind regain their sight, the lame walk, lepers are cleansed, the deaf hear, the dead are raised, the poor have the good news proclaimed to them. And blessed is the one who takes no offense at me."

— LUKE 7:18B–23

TODAY JESUS TELLS US that we are blessed if we are not offended by him. We might think there's no chance of being offended by God, but in reality, we are offended by Jesus more often than we realize. The Incarnation is an affront to a heart colored by the sin of pride. From the moment he is born, Christ calls us on a path that offends us. As a child, his tiny, helpless body was laid in a dirty manger and wrapped in cloths heavy with the dust of travel. As a man, his scourged body was thrown

Morire a se stessi (Die to Self), Kreg Yingst, @psalmprayers.

95

on a cross and nailed to it, ribs heaving, the stench of sweat intermingling with dirt and blood. We may prefer to think we are just observers of these scenes, but Jesus calls us to join him, from the itchy straw of the manger to the splintered Cross on Golgotha, the Place of the Skull. He calls us to follow him in a spirit of humble obedience to the Father's will.

This way of life, the way of Jesus, is not as simple and unoffensive as we might tend to think. "Take up your cross daily" (see Lk 9:23) are words none of us want to hear. So when we are offended by this call to holiness, we might turn away from the suffering and joy of faith to seek consolation in forgetfulness, bodily pleasures, and distractions. If we notice we are doing this, we can be honest with God and call out in prayer: "Yes, Jesus, I am offended by your Incarnation, by your suffering, by your death! Unlike Mary, I cannot find joy in life's suffering. I am offended by what you ask of me in following you! Sometimes I am offended by the idea of hell more than I am grateful that I have been saved from it! Jesus, help me not to be offended by you. Help me to embrace the tension of our faith's paradoxes, instead of picking and choosing the aspects of our faith that make me comfortable. Help me to die to myself so that, like your Mother, I may find joy and true comfort in you, in this life and in the next."

Examen *(see p. 153)*

Many sorrows and woes await the miserable person who puts desire, heart, and hope in earthly things, thereby forsaking and losing heavenly things and finally losing even earthly things as well. The eagle soars very high but if she tied a weight to her wings, she would not be able to fly very high. Similarly, because of the weight of earthly things a person cannot fly high or attain perfection. However, the wise person who binds the weight of the remembrance of death and judgment to the wings of his heart will not go astray nor fly at the vanities nor riches of this world, which are a cause of damnation.

Every day we see worldly people toil much and encounter great bodily perils to gain false riches. And after they have toiled and gained much, in a moment they die and leave behind all they gained in their lives.

Therefore, do not put your trust in this false world that beguiles, for it is a liar. But whoever desires to be great and truly rich, let them seek after and love everlasting riches and good things, that ever savor sweetly and never satiate and never grow less. If we would not go astray, let us take pattern from the beasts and the birds, for these, when they are fed, are content and seek not their living save from hour to hour when their need comes. Similarly, we should be content with satisfying our needs temperately, and not seek after superfluities.

Friar Giles said that the ant was not as pleasing to Saint Francis as other living things because of the great diligence she has in gathering together and storing up, in the time of summer, a treasure of grain for the winter. But he would say that the birds pleased him much more, because they laid not up one day for the next. Yet the ant teaches us that we ought not be slothful in the summer of this present life, so that we may not be found empty and barren in the winter of the last day and judgment.

— *The Little Flowers of Saint Francis* (Chapter VII)

Journaling and Prayer

Imagine you are resting your head against Jesus' manger. The Infant Jesus is laughing, then crying. Pooping and eating. Are you offended by Jesus' humanity? By his love? By his frailty? Search your heart for what offends you. What aspects of the faith are offensive to you? Do you resist any of the sacraments? Any of the teachings of the Church? Ask Jesus for the grace and humility not to be offended by him.

Third Thursday of Advent

READINGS: Is 54:1–10 / Ps 30:2–4, 5–6, 11–12a–13b / Lk 7:24–30

When the messengers of John had left, Jesus began to speak to the crowds about John. "What did you go out to the desert to see—a reed swayed by the wind? Then what did you go out to see? Someone dressed in fine garments? Those who dress luxuriously and live sumptuously are found in royal palaces. Then what did you go out to see? A prophet? Yes, I tell you, and more than a prophet. This is the one about whom scripture says:

'Behold, I am sending my messenger ahead of you,
he will prepare your way before you.'

I tell you, among those born of women, no one is greater than John; yet the least in the kingdom of God is greater than he."

— LUKE 7:24–30

IN TODAY'S GOSPEL JESUS asks the people what they went out to see when they traveled to the desert to be baptized by John the Baptist. He asks if they went out to see a man in fine garments, a man who indulged in sumptuous living, a man who became so weak and fickle through his way of living that he would vacillate like a swaying reed. Of course, the people listening to Jesus already knew that John the Baptist was not this kind of man. Detached from earthly comforts and success, John the Baptist was not looking for people's admiration. He lived in truth and rejected evil with the forcefulness of all his being. Anyone who glimpsed John the Baptist for a moment knew this immediately about him. The way he lived his life was stunning at the time, and even now, two thousand years later, it still surprises and inspires us.

Jesus asks questions about John's way of life to point us to reflect on the supernatural, grace-filled life John led. Saint John Chrysostom once wrote, "[John the Baptist] lived as though he were in heaven." But what could that mean? Heaven is compared in Scripture to a feast and a banquet and John ate locusts (see Mt 3:4) and lived in the desert! Is that not hell rather than heaven? Not for the saint. The saints live heaven, sometimes in the midst of hellish circumstances, because union with Christ is their main priority. Not money, not power, not sensuality—only Jesus. John the Baptist never received sacramental Baptism. But he is believed to have been sanctified in the womb of his mother and thus lived a baptismal communion with God. John's soul was then a foretaste of heaven, a tabernacle reserved only for God. Like Mary, the Cause of Our Joy, John lived in union with the cause of his being, God himself. Through frequent reception of the sacraments, we too can strive to be evermore rooted in the baptismal presence of God within our souls. Like John the Baptist, even amid earth's sometimes hellish sufferings, we can begin to live heaven now.

Examen *(see p. 153)*

O how good is God! O how good and how powerful is the Lord! He gives not only advice, but remedies also. His words are works. How our faith is thus strengthened and our love increased! Thus, I often call to mind how our Lord, when a tempest had risen at sea, commanded the winds and the waves, and there came a great calm; and I used to say then, "Who is this whom all the powers of my soul obey, and who in an instant gives such dazzling light to chase away such great darkness, and makes that heart become soft which seemed before to be as hard as a stone, and who gives the water of sweet tears, where before there was so long such a great drought? Who inspires these desires? Who gives such courage? What have I been thinking of that I should fear? What is this desire to serve this Lord?"

I wish for nothing but to please God. I renounce all pleasure, and ease, and every other good, save only the doing of his will, and of this good I was sure, as I can easily affirm. Since then this Lord is so powerful, as I see he is, and know he is, and since all the devils are his slaves (and of this I can have no doubt, since it is of faith), what harm can they do me, a servant of this Lord and King? Why shouldn't I have the strength to fight with all the powers of hell?

— Saint Teresa of Avila, *The Life of Teresa of Jesus*

Journaling and Prayer

Spend some time in your imagination with John the Baptist. Observe him throughout his day. Engage in conversation with him and ask for his intercession for your life, that you may live more for heaven no matter your circumstances. Are you living for heaven now? Is there a time in your life when you were not? What was your state of mind compared to times when you are living a life closer to Christ?

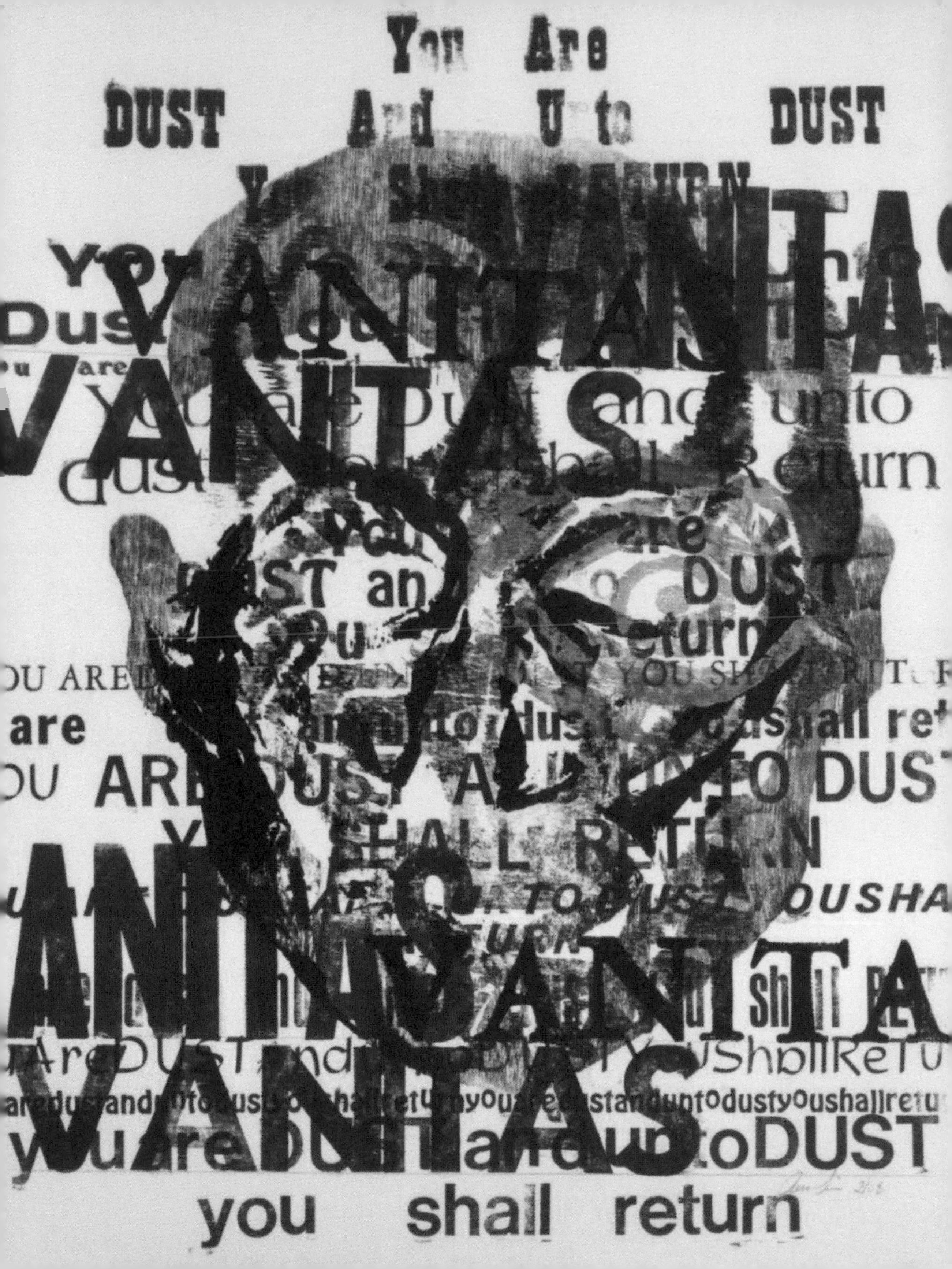
You Are
DUST
DUST
VANITAS
unto
Return
DUST
are
DUST
TO DUST
VANITAS
toDUST
you shall return

Third Friday of Advent

READINGS: Is 56:1–3a, 6–8 / Ps 67:2–3, 5, 7–8 / Jn 5:33–36

[Jesus said,] "You sent emissaries to John, and he testified to the truth. I do not accept testimony from a human being, but I say this so that you may be saved. He was a burning and shining lamp, and for a while you were content to rejoice in his light. But I have testimony greater than John's. The works that the Father gave me to accomplish, these works that I perform testify on my behalf that the Father has sent me."

— JOHN 5:33–36

JESUS TELLS US IN today's Gospel that he does not accept testimony from a human being "so that [we] might be saved." But why wouldn't Jesus accept the testimony of John, whom Jesus acknowledges as "a burning and shining lamp"? Because while John is a lamp, Jesus is the source of all light, the burning, shining Sun, the center and pinnacle of the universe. Jesus is the Truth; John merely came to testify to the Truth. Saint Hildegard of Bingen described John the Baptist as a man who "glittered with miracles in his faithful and serene deeds." He glittered because the light of Jesus Truth burned him like a thousand suns. And John allowed the light of Truth to burn away everything that distracted him from his mission.

Vanitas, Anna Griebe, @anna_luisamarie.

When meditating on the Last Things, we can learn from John the Baptist's example. He shows us that by submitting ourselves as living sacrifices (see Rom 12:1) to burn in the fire of God's Truth, we avoid eternal fire. As we submit to God's gentle fire of Truth, it burns away our complacencies, wasteful pleasures, unnecessary indulgences, lack of charity, and pride. When we allow Jesus Truth to come close to the everyday details of our lives, he purifies us so that we might become like gold tested by fire (see 1 Pt 1:7). In this process we are transformed from merely reflecting the light, to allowing Jesus to burn more brightly both within and through us. Saint Robert Bellarmine wrote that one "cannot directly fix the eye of his soul upon God, who is the light, without being enlightened by him." When we allow Jesus to continually light our baptismal fire through the grace of the other sacraments, our every step becomes fire. We become like John the Baptist, burning, shining lamps that bring God's light with us everywhere we go.

Examen *(see p. 153)*

[God the Father, speaking to Saint Catherine of Siena]: I am that Fire that purifies the soul. The closer the soul is to me, the purer she becomes. And the further she is from me, the more does her purity leave her, which is the reason why people of the world fall into such iniquities, for they are separated from me, while the soul who without any medium unites herself directly to me participates in my purity. Another thing is necessary for you to arrive at this union and purity, namely, that . . . my will alone should you consider, both in others and in yourself. And, if you should see evident sins or defects, draw out of those thorns the rose, that is to say, offer them to me, with holy compassion.

In the case of injuries done to yourself, judge that my will permits this in order to prove virtue in you, and in my other servants, esteeming that the person who acts thus does so as the instrument of my will; perceiving, moreover, that such apparent sinners may frequently have a good intention, for no one can judge the secrets of the heart. That which you do not see you should not judge in your mind, even though it may externally be open mortal sin, seeing nothing in others but my will, not in order to judge, but, as has been said, with holy compassion. In this way you will arrive at perfect purity, because acting thus, your mind will not be scandalized, either in me or in your neighbor.

Otherwise, you fall into contempt of your neighbor, if you judge his evil will toward you, instead of my will acting in him. Such contempt and scandal separate the soul from me, and prevent perfection, and, in some cases, deprive a person of grace, more or less according to the gravity of his contempt and the hatred which his judgment has conceived against his neighbor. A different reward is received by the soul who perceives only my will, which, as has been said, wishes nothing else but your good; so that everything which I give or permit to happen to you, I give so that you may arrive at the end for which I created you. And because the soul remains always in the love of her neighbor, she remains always in mine, and thus remains united to me.

Wherefore, in order to arrive at purity, you must entreat me to do three things: to grant you to be united to me by the affection of love, retaining in your memory the benefits you have received from me; and with the eye of your intellect to see the affection of my love, with which I love you inestimably; and in the will of others to discern my will only, and not their evil will, for I am their Judge, not you, and, in doing this, you will arrive at all perfection.

— Saint Catherine of Siena, *The Dialogue*

Journaling and Prayer

Close your eyes and think of a time in your life when you felt "burned" by God's fire of truth. Ask God to help you to see how you grew from his purifying action. Why do you think spiritual growth is painful? How does it prepare you for heaven?

The third Saturday of Advent always falls on or after December 17, so the reflection for this day can be found according to the current date.

FOURTH WEEK OF ADVENT

HEAVEN

During Advent and Christmas, we hear such expressions as "Love is born" or "the Incarnation of Jesus is when heaven meets earth." But we can easily file these away as trite phrases that don't directly impact our lives. Though Scripture assures us that God is love (see 1 Jn 4:8) and we know we will meet God in heaven, we might still wonder what these words mean concretely. After all, both "heaven" and "love" are words bandied about in popular culture in ways that drain them almost completely of meaning. Yes, God is love, and heaven meets earth in the Incarnation. But what does this actually mean? In order to understand these phrases more fully and come to a deeper understanding of the true meaning of the Incarnation and heaven, it's helpful to contemplate the mystery of God in view of these assurances.

Saint Thomas Aquinas helps us to contemplate God in this way in the first part of the *Summa Theologiae*. There he describes the unknowability and otherness of God using our reason alone: "We cannot know what God is, but only what he is not" (ST I–I). In other words, because God is greater than what we can know, comprehend, or understand, he cannot be fully understood: God is more unlike all we can know than he is like it. When we understand who God is in this way, or more accurately who he is not, our meditation on heaven, and the Incarnation, changes. We begin to more fully understand that the transcendent second Person of the Trinity, the Son of God, became incarnate so that we might know God and be saved. It's a mystery that defies simplistic sentimentalism and reductive phrases.

Meditating on heaven, therefore, is a meditation on our transcendent God, not a meditation on chubby cherubs and cotton-candy clouds. Heaven is union with the One whom we cannot comprehend now in his being and his mystery, but whom we can know more fully in his Incarnation. By revealing himself to us, Jesus has given us a glimpse of our heavenly Father, and a preview of the joy of eternal union with God in heaven: "[Christ] is the image of the invisible God" (Col 1:15). When we think of the astonishing descent that the Son of God took upon himself in order to become human, live, suffer, die, and rise so that he may open the doors of heaven for us, we begin to realize more fully the astounding mystery of the Nativity of Jesus.

How then can we prepare ourselves for heaven—for God—these last days of Advent? We can contemplate the transcendence of God, whose nature we cannot even fathom, and how he has deigned to reveal himself to us in the Incarnation. We can draw near to Jesus, this God-child, in the manger. Indeed, the Son of God became a child so that we may draw near to him. We can draw near to him not just in our imagination but concretely in the Church, in the sacraments, in Scripture. We meditate on heaven and draw closer to God when we read the word of God, when we converse with him in prayer, and when we receive Jesus' Body, Blood, Soul, and Divinity in the Eucharist at Mass.

Indeed, all the sacraments are glimpses of heaven that prepare us for the end of our lives. But reception of the Eucharist in particular makes efficacious our meditation on the Last Things, as it trains our desires away from the passing things of this world and toward heaven. Communion is a remedy and a weapon against concupiscence in the spiritual life. This powerful source of grace unites us with God, preserving, increasing, and renewing our baptismal grace. By receiving the Eucharist regularly, we unite ourselves to the Incarnate Christ and to his way of life. Saint Cyril of Alexandria describes this process as "when melted wax is fused with other wax." Meditation on heaven, therefore, is a way that we can enter more fully into the unfathomable happiness that we begin to taste in the sacraments and will experience even more deeply when we meet God face to face, this God who loves us beyond measure.

> By his death and resurrection, Jesus Christ has "opened" heaven to us. The life of the blessed consists in the full and perfect possession of the fruits of the redemption accomplished by Christ. He makes partners in his heavenly glorification those who have believed in him and remained faithful to his will. Heaven is the blessed community of all who are perfectly incorporated into Christ.
>
> This mystery of blessed communion with God and all who are in Christ is beyond all understanding and description. Scripture speaks of it in

images: life, light, peace, wedding feast, wine of the kingdom, the Father's house, the heavenly Jerusalem, paradise: "no eye has seen, nor ear heard, nor the heart of man conceived, what God has prepared for those who love him" [1 Cor 2:9].

Because of his transcendence, God cannot be seen as he is, unless he himself opens up his mystery to man's immediate contemplation and gives him the capacity for it. The Church calls this contemplation of God in his heavenly glory "the beatific vision":

> How great will your glory and happiness be, to be allowed to see God, to be honored with sharing the joy of salvation and eternal light with Christ your Lord and God . . . to delight in the joy of immortality in the Kingdom of heaven with the righteous and God's friends [Saint Cyprian, Epistle 58, 10, 1].

— *Catechism of the Catholic Church* (nos. 1026–1028)

NOTHING WILL BE ABLE TO SEPARATE US FROM HIS LOVE

ROMANS 8:39

Fourth Sunday of Advent

YEAR A: Is 7:10–14 / Ps 24:1–2, 3–4, 5–6 / Rom 1:1–7 / Mt 1:18–24

YEAR B: 2 Sm 7:1–5, 8b–12, 14a, 16 / Ps 89:2–3, 4–5, 27, 29 / Rom 16:25–27 / Lk 1:26–38

YEAR C: Mi 5:1–4a, Ps 80:2–3, 15–16, 18–19 / Heb 10:5–10 / Lk 1:39–45

The angel of the Lord appeared to him in a dream and said, "Joseph, son of David, do not be afraid to take Mary your wife into your home. For it is through the holy Spirit that this child has been conceived in her. She will bear a son and you are to name him Jesus, because he will save his people from their sins." All this took place to fulfill what the Lord had said through the prophet:

> "Behold, the virgin shall be with child and bear a son,
> and they shall name him Emmanuel,"
> which means "God is with us."

— MATTHEW 1:20–23

In the sixth month, the angel Gabriel was sent from God to a town of Galilee called Nazareth, to a virgin betrothed to a man named Joseph, of the house of David, and the virgin's name was Mary. And coming to her, he said, "Hail, favored one! The Lord is with you."

— LUKE 1:26–28

During those days Mary set out and traveled to the hill country in haste to a town of Judah, where she entered the house of Zechariah and greeted Elizabeth. When Elizabeth heard Mary's greeting, the infant

Heavenly Stems and Earthly Branches,
David Noble, @ignoble_one.

leaped in her womb, and Elizabeth, filled with the holy Spirit, cried out in a loud voice and said, "Most blessed are you among women, and blessed is the fruit of your womb.

— Luke 1:39–42

GOD VISITS HIS PEOPLE in the Incarnation. All three possible Gospels for this Sunday speak of these visits. In the Gospel of Matthew, we are told that Jesus' birth fulfills the prophecy of a child to be born who will be named Emmanuel, meaning "God is with us." In the Gospel of Luke, Gabriel greets Mary by saying, "The Lord is with you." Then, Mary carries God-in-the-flesh as a fetus in her womb to see her cousin Elizabeth. These moments communicate to us that though the God of Scripture is transcendent and "other," he is not a distant God who sets himself apart. God comes to visit his people; he is actively present in the lives of his people. We see God do this throughout the Old Testament in symbolic ways, "theophanies" or manifestations of his presence in things like fire, pillars of smoke, or a burning bush. But in the miracle of the Incarnation, God's presence to his people surpasses all previous visitations as the second Person of the Trinity, the Son of God, becomes human.

From the very beginning of the Incarnation, Mary shows us how God often chooses to depend on human beings in salvation history to bring his presence to others. She carries the divine presence within her, not just in her womb for nine months but in all the words, actions, and events of her life. Like Mary, we too are called to carry this presence of God to others. While we do not carry the child Jesus and give birth to him in a literal sense as Mary did, we do carry the baptismal presence of the Trinity dwelling within us. We might think this comparison abstract, but it's far more real than it might seem. Since God dwells in us through our Baptism, in some sense we carry heaven within us now. As Saint Elizabeth of the Trinity once wrote, "I have found my heaven on earth, since heaven is God, and God is [in] my soul." Like Mary, we too give birth to Jesus in our lives if we continually ask for the grace to unite ourselves ever more with the indwelling presence of the Trinity within us. As we follow Mary's example in these last days of Advent, may she help us learn to be attentive to God's indwelling presence with the gentle care and fierce protectiveness of a mother who knows the treasure she carries within her.

Examen *(see p. 153)*

I need make no effort to enter into the mystery of God dwelling within the Blessed Virgin; it seems to resemble my usual attitude of soul, and like her, I adore the hidden God within me. When I read in the Gospel that Mary went in haste to the mountains of Judea on her charitable mission to her cousin Elizabeth, I can see her as she passes, calm, majestic, recollected, holding commune within herself with the Word of God.

Her prayer was always the same as his: "*Ecce*, here I am." Who? The handmaid of the Lord, his mother, the lowliest of all creatures. Her humility was sincere because she was always forgetful of self, unconscious of, freed from self, so that she could sing, "From henceforth all generations shall call me blessed. Because he that is mighty has done great things to me."

— Saint Elizabeth of the Trinity, *Last Retreat*

Journaling and Prayer

Recall a time you felt especially loved by God through another person. Sit for some time recalling that person's love and absorbing it into your heart, mind, and soul. Thank God for loving you through that person. What are some ways God has provided you with love from others to make up for a lack of love in your life, or some ways you have encountered God's love through prayer? What are some concrete ways that you can also bring Jesus' love to others?

December 17

Readings: Gn 49:2, 8–10 / Ps 72:1–2, 3–4ab, 7–8, 17 / Mt 1:1–17

The book of the genealogy of Jesus Christ, the son of David, the son of Abraham.

Abraham became the father of Isaac, Isaac the father of Jacob, Jacob the father of Judah and his brothers. Judah became the father of Perez and Zerah, whose mother was Tamar. Perez became the father of Hezron, Hezron the father of Ram, Ram the father of Amminadab. Amminadab became the father of Nahshon, Nahshon the father of Salmon, Salmon the father of Boaz, whose mother was Rahab. Boaz became the father of Obed, whose mother was Ruth. Obed became the father of Jesse, Jesse the father of David the king.

David became the father of Solomon, whose mother had been the wife of Uriah. Solomon became the father of Rehoboam, Rehoboam the father of Abijah, Abijah the father of Asaph. Asaph became the father of Jehoshaphat, Jehoshaphat the father of Joram, Joram the father of Uzziah. Uzziah became the father of Jotham, Jotham the father of Ahaz, Ahaz the father of Hezekiah. Hezekiah became the father of Manasseh, Manasseh the father of Amos, Amos the father of Josiah. Josiah became the father of Jechoniah and his brothers at the time of the Babylonian exile.

After the Babylonian exile, Jechoniah became the father of Shealtiel, Shealtiel the father of Zerubbabel, Zerubbabel the father of Abiud. Abiud

After That Comes Judgment, Jeremy Stout, @jstoutillustration.

became the father of Eliakim, Eliakim the father of Azor, Azor the father of
Zadok. Zadok became the father of Achim, Achim the father of Eliud, Eliud
the father of Eleazar. Eleazar became the father of Matthan, Matthan the
father of Jacob, Jacob the father of Joseph, the husband of Mary. Of her
was born Jesus who is called the Messiah.

— Matthew 1:1–16

THE GENEALOGY OF JESUS can seem like a dry recitation of names that
disappear like ashes in the wind as we say them. But it only seems so if
we are not paying attention to how God works. Just as each of our lives
depend on the lives and deaths of generations before us, so did the
humanity of Jesus. As each person in the line of David died, the world
stepped closer to the Incarnation of God. The litany of names in today's
Gospel is like a string of pearls that lead to the pearl of great price: Jesus
Christ (Mt 13:45–46). Unlike most genealogical litanies, however, the
death of those before Jesus did not lead to just another death in a long
generational chain. Jesus halted the usual pattern of life and death followed by life and death. Indeed, a pearl unlike all others, he lived, then
died—then rose again.

Jesus' death is the only death in human history in which death itself
was conquered. His death led to life, not just his own in the resurrection,
but that of humanity. Because of Jesus, the life of every Christian in the
generational chain of life is fundamentally changed. Because of Jesus,
our death now leads to life, to the treasure of the beatific vision in heaven
and the resurrection of the body. Therefore, we can be confident that
even in our human experiences of death, grief, existential angst, and
doubt, Jesus is our hope. With him, life exists beyond death. With Jesus
is found unfathomable joy and rest. So even when darkness descends
and we temporarily lose sight of this truth, we can remind ourselves that
we each have a place in a glimmering string of pearls that stretches into
heaven. Our death, like the deaths of the men and women in the line of
David, will lead to the pearl of great price: Jesus.

Examen *(see p. 153)*

What do you seek? Or what does everyone who seeks find? I venture to answer, pearls; and the pearl that a person possesses, who has given up all things and counted them as loss [is] Christ, the one very precious pearl. Precious, then, is a lamp to those in darkness, and there is need of a lamp until the sunrise. And precious also is the glory in the face of Moses, and of the prophets also, and a beautiful sight, by which we are introduced so as to be able to see the glory of Christ, to which the Father bears witness, saying, "This is my beloved Son in whom I am well-pleased" (Mt 3:17). . . .

Every soul, therefore, which comes to childhood and is on the way to full growth, until the fullness of time is at hand, needs a tutor and stewards and guardians, in order that, after all these things . . . when freed from a tutor and stewards and guardians, each person may receive the patrimony corresponding to the very costly pearl. . . . "To everything then is its season, and a time for everything under heaven" (Eccl 3:1), a time to gather the goodly pearls, and a time after their gathering to find the one precious pearl, when it is fitting for a person to go away and sell all he has in order that he may buy that pearl.

— Origen, *Commentary on Matthew*

Journaling and Prayer

The life-giving power of faith is often passed down to us through family tradition and belief. Recall any deceased family members who contributed to your life of faith. Recall concrete events when they taught you something about God and the faith. Thank God for that person's impact on your life and pray that faith may continue in your family line. How are you called to share the faith within your family?

December 18

READINGS: Jer 23:5–8 / Ps 72:1–2, 12–13, 18–19 / Mt 1:18–24

Now this is how the birth of Jesus Christ came about. When his mother Mary was betrothed to Joseph, but before they lived together, she was found with child through the holy Spirit. Joseph, her husband, since he was a righteous man, yet unwilling to expose her to shame, decided to divorce her quietly. Such was his intention when, behold, the angel of the Lord appeared to him in a dream and said, "Joseph, son of David, do not be afraid to take Mary your wife into your home. For it is through the holy Spirit that this child has been conceived in her. She will bear a son and you are to name him Jesus, because he will save his people from their sins." All this took place to fulfill what the Lord had said through the prophet:

"Behold, the virgin shall be with child and bear a son,
    and they shall name him Emmanuel,"

which means "God is with us." When Joseph awoke, he did as the angel of the Lord had commanded him and took his wife into his home.

— MATTHEW 1:18–24

Death of Saint Joseph, James Langley, @langley.artgram.

WE OFTEN TAKE THE events of Scripture for granted. After reading today's Gospel, for example, we might think, "Of course Joseph obeyed the angel who appeared to him in a dream." But if God sent an angel to tell us something in our dreams, how many of us would wake up and immediately take steps that would completely change our lives? Wouldn't most of us instead wake up and say, "What a strange dream. Oh well. Anyway, what is on today's to-do list?" When we really consider what happened in today's Gospel and let the fruit of our reflection enter our lives, Joseph's obedience will astonish and change us. Attuned to the ways of God, Joseph acted in the strength and trust of someone who knows God's power. Before Jesus was even born, Joseph modeled his Son's obedience to the Father's will.

During Advent, as we meditate on the joy awaiting us in heaven, it's also beneficial to meditate on Joseph's obedience. His life shows us that the key to open heaven's door is an obedient heart that follows God's will. Reflection on Saint Joseph's obedience can be a remedy for the prideful disobedience that leads us to resist death. Such an attitude of disobedience can cause us to focus inordinately on what we see as the negative aspects of the Last Things rather than on heaven. The mystery of Christ's incarnation, death, and resurrection calls forth a response of ecstatic joy, but in order to respond with joy we must first listen to God and grow in obedient trust. Preparing for heaven involves cultivating a heart like the heart of Saint Joseph—obedient even unto death. Hearts like Saint Joseph's see that death, the final consequence of sin, has been transformed by Christ into a gold-gilded doorway to heaven!

Examen (see p. 153)

(see p. 153)

> We should be particularly devout to Saint Joseph, that he may obtain for us a happy death. Because he preserved the child Jesus from the snares of his enemies, he has the particular privilege of delivering those who are dying from the snares of the devil. Also, because of the assistance that he rendered for so many years to Jesus and to Mary in providing them by his own labor with food and lodging, he has the privilege of obtaining for

those who are devout to him at the time of their death a particular assistance from Jesus and Mary.

My holy protector, Saint Joseph, by my sins I have deserved an evil death; but if you defend me, I shall not be lost. You have not only been a great friend of my Judge, but also his guardian and foster father; recommend me therefore to your divine Jesus, who so much loves you. I place myself under your protection; accept me for your constant servant. And through that holy company which you enjoyed in the life of Jesus and Mary, obtain for me from God that I may never be separated from their love. And through the assistance which Jesus and Mary rendered you at your death, obtain for me a particular assistance at the hour of my death, from Jesus and Mary. Holy Virgin, through the love which you cherished toward your spouse Joseph, fail not to assist me at the hour of my death.

— Saint Alphonsus Liguori, *The Way of Salvation*

Journaling and Prayer

Imagine Saint Joseph waking up from one of his dreams in which an angel spoke to him. Observe his thoughts, his attitude, his desires. Walk around the room with him as he wonders aloud about what has just happened. What do you notice? What is inspiring to you about Saint Joseph's disposition and response? How can you be more like him?

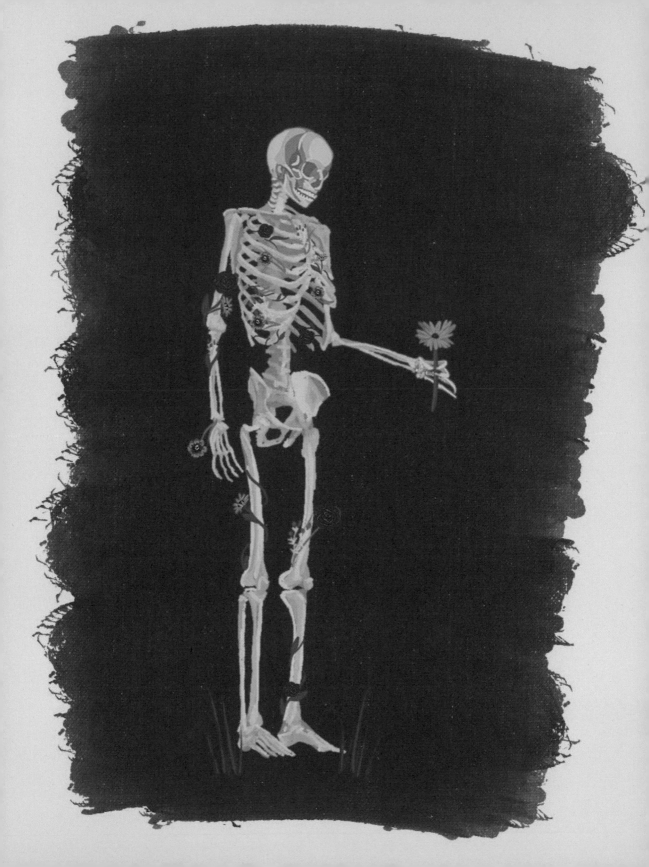

December 19

Readings: Jgs 13:2–7, 24–25a / Ps 71:3–4a, 5–6ab, 16–17 / Lk 1:5–25

In the days of Herod, King of Judea, there was a priest named Zechariah of the priestly division of Abijah; his wife was from the daughters of Aaron, and her name was Elizabeth. Both were righteous in the eyes of God, observing all the commandments and ordinances of the Lord blamelessly. But they had no child, because Elizabeth was barren and both were advanced in years. Once when he was serving as priest in his division's turn before God, according to the practice of the priestly service, he was chosen by lot to enter the sanctuary of the Lord to burn incense. Then, when the whole assembly of the people was praying outside at the hour of the incense offering, the angel of the Lord appeared to him, standing at the right of the altar of incense. Zechariah was troubled by what he saw, and fear came upon him. But the angel said to him, "Do not be afraid, Zechariah, because your prayer has been heard. Your wife Elizabeth will bear you a son, and you shall name him John. And you will have joy and gladness, and many will rejoice at his birth, for he will be great in the sight of [the] Lord. He will drink neither wine nor strong drink. He will be filled with the holy Spirit even from his mother's womb, and he will turn many of the children of Israel to the Lord their God. He will go before him in the spirit and power of Elijah to turn the hearts of fathers toward children and the disobedient to the understanding of the righteous, to prepare a people fit for the Lord." Then Zechariah said to the angel, "How shall I know

You Turn Graves into Gardens, Valerie Delgado, @pax.valerie.

this? For I am an old man, and my wife is advanced in years." And the angel said to him in reply, "I am Gabriel, who stand before God. I was sent to speak to you and to announce to you this good news. But now you will be speechless and unable to talk until the day these things take place, because you did not believe my words, which will be fulfilled at their proper time."

— LUKE 1:5–20

THE ANGEL GABRIEL REACTS very differently to Zechariah's and Mary's responses to his announcements in Scripture. He praises Mary and harshly chastises Zechariah. Yet the difference between Mary's and Zechariah's reactions to the two annunciations is not immediately discernible. Both seem to respond with fear and doubt to the angel's good news. The difference, however, lies in the fact that whereas Mary's reaction to the annunciation moves through these normal human emotions and ends in trust, Zechariah's does not. He remains in the chaotic storm of his initial reaction and does not trust in the grace of God to move him further. For this, Zechariah is rendered unable to speak until John the Baptist is born.

Zechariah was not made temporarily mute because he had an understandable reaction to an angel appearing in all its glory and terror before him. Instead he was made mute for not allowing God's grace to correct and reign above his natural human response. When we meditate on the Last Things, it can help to remember that we will naturally experience a range of emotions, just as Zechariah and Mary did. But like Mary we can allow supernatural grace to propel us through difficult feelings so that we might ultimately raise our eyes to heaven. After all, as Blessed James Alberione would often point out, exercises in preparation for death are really exercises in preparation for heaven. Meditation on heaven begins in meditation on death and the other Last Things, but with God's grace our meditation will end in trusting contemplation of heaven, the place where we will be freed from any kind of suffering and every tear will be wiped away (see Rev 21:4). Like Mary, we can trust this is possible because what is impossible for us is always possible for God (see Lk 18:27).

Examen *(see p. 153)*

Saint Mechtilde once asked the Blessed Virgin Mary to assist her in the hour of her death and was taught these three prayers:

Hail, Mary, full of grace, the Lord is with thee; blessed art thou among women, and blessed is the fruit of thy womb, Jesus. Holy Mary, Mother of God, as God the Father in the grandeur of his omnipotence has exalted you and given you power above all creatures, be with me, I beseech you, in the hour of my death, and drive far from me all the snares and craft of my enemies. Amen.

Hail, Mary, Holy Mary, Mother of God, as God the Son in the excellence of his unsearchable wisdom has imbued you with such great knowledge and filled you with such great light that you know the most Holy Trinity more truly and intimately than all saints, please enlighten my soul in the hour of my death with the knowledge of the faith, that no error or ignorance may lead it astray. Amen.

Hail, Mary, Holy Mary, Mother of God, as the Holy Spirit has poured into you the sweetness of his love with such abundance that you are, after God, the sweetest and most benign of beings, please pour into my soul at the hour of my death the sweetness of divine love so that its every bitterness may be rendered sweet to me. Amen.

— Saint Mechtilde, *Preces Gertrudianae*

Journaling and Prayer

Take a few minutes to meditate on heaven. Observe the thoughts, emotions, images, and concepts that come to your mind. Do they lead you to focus on other things besides heaven? If so, try to allow them to pass by as you ask God for the supernatural grace to meditate on heaven.

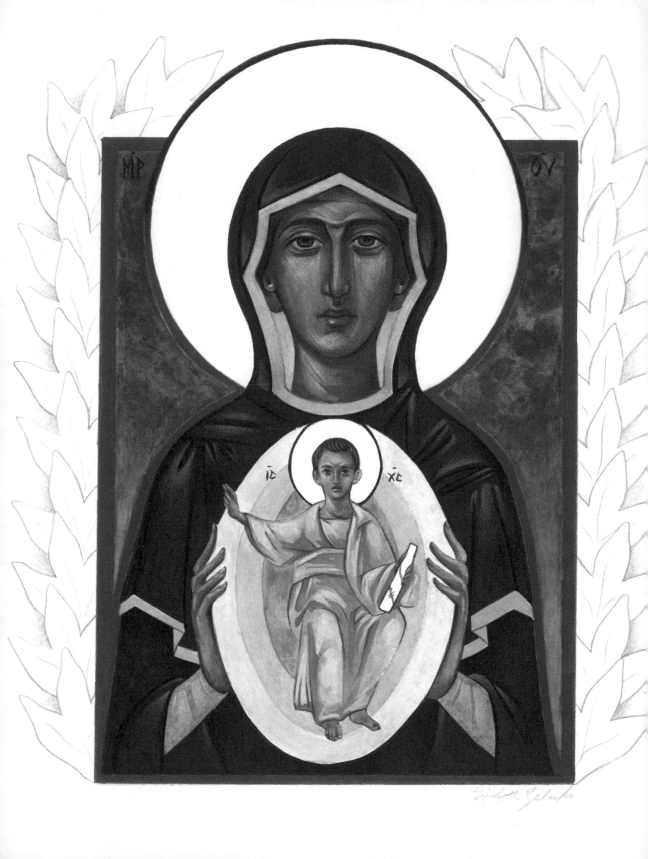

December 20

READINGS: Is 7:10–14 / Ps 24:1–2, 3–4ab, 5–6 / Lk 1:26–38

In the sixth month, the angel Gabriel was sent from God to a town of Galilee called Nazareth, to a virgin betrothed to a man named Joseph, of the house of David, and the virgin's name was Mary. And coming to her, he said, "Hail, favored one! The Lord is with you." But she was greatly troubled at what was said and pondered what sort of greeting this might be. Then the angel said to her, "Do not be afraid, Mary, for you have found favor with God. Behold, you will conceive in your womb and bear a son, and you shall name him Jesus. He will be great and will be called Son of the Most High, and the Lord God will give him the throne of David his father, and he will rule over the house of Jacob forever, and of his kingdom there will be no end." But Mary said to the angel, "How can this be, since I have no relations with a man?" And the angel said to her in reply, "The holy Spirit will come upon you, and the power of the Most High will overshadow you. Therefore the child to be born will be called holy, the Son of God. And behold, Elizabeth, your relative, has also conceived a son in her old age, and this is the sixth month for her who was called barren; for nothing will be impossible for God." Mary said, "Behold, I am the handmaid of the Lord. May it be done to me according to your word." Then the angel departed from her.

— Luke 1:26–38

Burning Bush, Elizabeth Zelasko, @elizabeth.zelasko.

WHEN MARY ASKS THE angel Gabriel how her situation is possible in today's Gospel, the phrase can be read in many ways. There are so many shades of possible emotions: doubtful, curious, skeptical, eager, awestruck. Perhaps Mary was expressing involuntary doubt in the moment? Or perhaps she believed Gabriel's message immediately and was amazed but confused? Or perhaps she was just not sure what to say? None of us know exactly what went through Mary's mind at that moment, but, whatever the truth of the situation, we do know one thing. Even with the terrifying figure of an angel before her, Mary had the presence of mind to ask for more information. Her relationship with God was such that she felt comfortable expressing, rather informally, her curiosity. What a refreshing moment in salvation history! Mary, the Mother of God, is curious and confused, and she shares her emotional reality with an angel of God.

Conversation with God, or prayer, will be different for each person, but we can learn from the open, humble sincerity of our Blessed Mother. The Lord wants to hear all that is on our minds and in our hearts. God wants us to relate with him as Mary related to the angel Gabriel. Jesus entered our human experience and has made us his friends (see Jn 15:15), and this friendship empowers us to openly share our thoughts, emotions, questions, and desires with him. The startling otherness of God, who created the heavens and the earth, gives the intimacy and friendship made possible through the Incarnation even more precious value. While meditation on the Last Things—even on heaven!—can seem intimidating, it doesn't have to be if we approach it like a conversation with the God who dwells within us and calls us his friends. In this context, meditation on heaven is simply a sincere, open conversation with a friend we trust, a friend who has laid down his life for us (see Jn 15:13), and who promises us a joyful reward in heaven (see Mt 5:12).

Examen (see p. 153)

[On the day of the Annunciation] strains of praise are sung joyfully by the choir of angels, and the light of the advent of Christ shines brightly upon the faithful. Today is like a glad springtime to us, and Christ the Sun of righteousness has beamed with clear light around us and illumined the minds of the faithful. . . .

Today Gabriel, who stands by God, did come to the pure virgin, bearing to her the glad annunciation, "Hail, you who are highly favored!" And she cast in her mind what manner of salutation this might be. And the angel immediately proceeded to say, "The Lord is with you: fear not, Mary; for you have found favor with God. Behold, you shall conceive in your womb, and bring forth a son, and shall call his name Jesus. . . ." Then said Mary to the angel, "How shall this be, seeing I know not a man?" . . . And while she was yet in perplexity as to these things, the angel placed shortly before her the summary of his whole message. . . .

Most of the holy fathers, and patriarchs, and prophets desired to see him, and to be eyewitnesses of him, but did not. And some of them by visions beheld him in type, and darkly; others, again, were privileged to hear the divine voice through the medium of the cloud and were favored with sights of holy angels. But to Mary the pure virgin alone did the archangel Gabriel manifest himself luminously, bringing her the glad address, "Hail, you who are highly favored!" And thus, she received the word and in the due time of the fulfillment . . . she brought forth the priceless pearl.

— Saint Gregory Thaumaturgus, *On the Annunciation to the Holy Virgin Mary*

Journaling and Prayer

Imagine yourself preparing a meal with Mary shortly after the Annunciation. Be with her and watch her as she teaches you about what she is preparing. Ask her how she was able to ask God such an honest question when the angel Gabriel appeared to her. Listen to her response and observe her face. What can you learn from Mary about being honest with God? Do you find this comes easily to you, or is it more difficult? Why?

LiLY OF THE VALLEY

MEMENTO MORI

December 21

READINGS: Sg 2:8–14 or Zep 3:14–18a / Ps 33:2–3, 11–12, 20–21 / Lk 1:39–45

During those days Mary set out and traveled to the hill country in haste to a town of Judah, where she entered the house of Zechariah and greeted Elizabeth. When Elizabeth heard Mary's greeting, the infant leaped in her womb, and Elizabeth, filled with the holy Spirit, cried out in a loud voice and said, "Most blessed are you among women, and blessed is the fruit of your womb. And how does this happen to me, that the mother of my Lord should come to me? For at the moment the sound of your greeting reached my ears, the infant in my womb leaped for joy. Blessed are you who believed that what was spoken to you by the Lord would be fulfilled."

— LUKE 1:39–45

AS A FAITHFUL JEW expectantly awaiting the arrival of the Messiah, Mary believed in God's promise of salvation for her people. Her holiness and focus on God must have been surprising even to the observant Jews around her. But much more surprising than her general belief in God's salvation was that she also believed the angel Gabriel when he announced to her that God would save her people very specifically through her. When Gabriel told her that she would bear the Son of God,

Our Lady of the Lunas, Christy Mandin, @christymandin.

she did not refuse or retreat into doubt; she said "yes." However improbable God's promise of salvation by way of her "yes" might have seemed to Mary, she believed because she believed in God's faithfulness and power—not in an abstract, general sense, but because God was real and personal to her.

Though we do not have the same role in salvation history as Mary, Jesus promises us salvation in a similarly personal way—not just for humanity in general but for us in particular. Jesus promises us that he is preparing a special place just for us in his Father's house, in heaven (see Jn 14:1–7). When we try to meditate on heaven, these kinds of Scripture passages may seem abstract or removed from our personal lives. But just as Mary knew that by her "yes" she was agreeing to a promise from God that was both real and concrete, we can trust that the promise of heaven we find in Scripture is similarly real and concrete for us personally. To understand this more fully, we can look to the mystery and gift of the sacraments, which are given to us in material things because God works through what he creates in order to encounter us. As Mary experienced the presence of Jesus in her womb in a real, concrete way, we similarly experience God's indwelling presence in our soul through the waters of Baptism. Amid life's unknowns, hardships, doubts, and fears, blessed are those who, like Mary, believe in God's promises of salvation and heaven. When we imitate Mary in her faithfulness, the angels and saints cry out, "Blessed are you who believed that what was spoken to you by the Lord would be fulfilled!"

Examen *(see p. 153)*

Letter to Mother Péronne Marie de Châtel, Superior at Grenoble:

You ask me, my dear daughter, if we are poor. Yes, indeed we are, but I hardly ever give it a thought. Heaven and earth may pass away, but the word of God remains eternally as the foundation of our hope. He has said that if we seek his kingdom and his justice all the rest shall be added unto us. I believe him, and I trust in him. The extreme necessity in which we sometimes find ourselves gives us opportunities to practice holy confidence in God and rare perfection. Truly we already see how wise it is to adhere to him and to hope in him against all human hope, for our foundation has been a thousand times more successful than we dared to anticipate.

— Saint Jane Frances de Chantal, *Letter (1619)*

Journaling and Prayer

Imagine yourself in the presence of Mary and the angel Gabriel at the Annunciation. Observe Mary's response to the angel's announcement, the movement of her feelings, and her faith-filled response. Do you believe God's promises as readily as Mary believed in the angel's promise? Ask Mary to help you to live, as she did, in faith-filled trust in God and in his real presence in you and in the world.

December 22

READINGS: 1 Sm 1:24–28 / 1 Sm 2:1, 4–5, 6–7, 8abcd / Lk 1:46–56

"My soul proclaims the greatness of the Lord;
    my spirit rejoices in God my savior.
For he has looked upon his handmaid's lowliness;
    behold, from now on will all ages call me blessed.
The Mighty One has done great things for me,
    and holy is his name.
His mercy is from age to age
    to those who fear him.
He has shown might with his arm,
    dispersed the arrogant of mind and heart.
He has thrown down the rulers from their thrones
    but lifted up the lowly.
The hungry he has filled with good things;
    the rich he has sent away empty.
He has helped Israel his servant,
    remembering his mercy,
according to his promise to our fathers,
    to Abraham and to his descendants forever."

— LUKE 1:46–55

The Annunciation of the Death of the Virgin,
Samuel van Hoogstraten (ca. 1670).

BEFORE THE SON OF God came to dwell in her womb, Mary united her soul to God in constant prayer. This allowed her to live in the presence of God in a contemplative stance toward the world and those around her. In this way Mary began to live heaven on earth, even before Jesus was incarnated within her. Then as Jesus grew in her womb, she was united to God in both soul and body. After Jesus was born and made his way slowly to Calvary, Mary continued to follow her Son without hesitation. For her entire life Mary united herself to God's love and pondered everything that she, her Son, or anyone else experienced in the context of this love. Her intense union with God imbued her with a faith that gave her confidence even in the bleakness of life's suffering.

Mary knew that no suffering, no evil, and no tragedy ever supersedes the love of God. She knew this on the deepest level of her being and clung to God's love in both the joys and sufferings of her life. On the fateful day when she followed her Son to Calvary, Mary's heavy heart continued to sing the words she sang to her cousin Elizabeth when she was pregnant with Jesus, "My soul proclaims the greatness of the Lord." As she gazed on her dying Son on the wood of the Cross, she remembered how she had gazed on him in the manger. And even in this moment Mary held the mystery of the darkness of sin and suffering up against the setting of God's love in her heart. Mary's union with God gave her the faith she needed to trust that God would bring about a great good for humanity through her Son's death. And though we have no testimony to it in Scripture, her example of strength in suffering must have continued even to the point of embracing her own death, in trust, like her Son. Like Mary, when we are faced with the darkness of the cross, of our suffering, and of our death, we too can hold it all up to the dazzling light of our final destination in God. Against the astounding backdrop of heaven, everything else will fade into insignificance.

Examen *(see p. 153)*

We cannot imagine [Mary] died any other death than that of love, the noblest death, a most fit end for the noblest life ever created, a death which angels would crave could they die. The early Christians loved each other so well that they "were of one heart and one soul" (Acts 4:32) and Saint Paul said that he no longer lived but Jesus Christ lived in him through the closeness of union whereby his heart was knit to his Redeemer's heart (see Gal 2:20). Surely, how much more must the Holy Virgin and her Son have had but one heart and one soul and one life? So the Blessed Mother lived not herself, but her Son lived in her, [for] love of a mother and her only son is among the greatest of earthly loves. And this was the love of a Mother unlike all other mothers, inasmuch as no earthly father had part in the birth of her Divine Son, and therefore their union was of a sort unlike all else. . . .

And if this Mother lived in her Son's life, surely she died in his death. We are told that the phoenix, growing old, gathers together on a mountaintop a pile of aromatic wood, and when the sun's rays are at the hottest, it beats its wings until the wood kindles and the bird is consumed amid the flames. Similarly, the Virgin Mother, having tenderly gathered and pondered in her memory all the mysteries of her Son's life and death, and receiving the brightest rays that he the Sun of Righteousness ever has shed upon any created in his love, fanning such flames with the breeze of her devout contemplation, surely at length heavenly love must have consumed her as a living sacrifice, and she must have rendered up her soul into her Son's arms. O blessed, life-giving death! O holy love, which through death leads to life!

— Saint Francis de Sales, *Treatise on the Love of God*

Journaling and Prayer

Recite the Magnificat, the prayer Mary says in today's Gospel. In your prayer take some time repeating a line or phrase from the Magnificat that you feel is personally significant. What does it say to you? What did Mary mean when she said it? What do you mean? How does it apply to your life as you are preparing for Christmas? How could it help you also prepare for heaven?

December 23

READINGS: Mal 3:1–4, 23–24 / Ps 25:4–5ab, 8–9, 10–14 / Lk 1:57–66

When the time arrived for Elizabeth to have her child she gave birth to a son. Her neighbors and relatives heard that the Lord had shown his great mercy toward her, and they rejoiced with her. When they came on the eighth day to circumcise the child, they were going to call him Zechariah after his father, but his mother said in reply, "No. He will be called John." But they answered her, "There is no one among your relatives who has this name." So they made signs, asking his father what he wished him to be called. He asked for a tablet and wrote, "John is his name," and all were amazed. Immediately his mouth was opened, his tongue freed, and he spoke blessing God. Then fear came upon all their neighbors, and all these matters were discussed throughout the hill country of Judea. All who heard these things took them to heart, saying, "What, then, will this child be? For surely the hand of the Lord was with him."

— LUKE 1:57–66

EVERYONE PRESENT AT THE birth of John the Baptist knew that he would have a special mission. The moment he was born, the people knew the hand of the Lord was with him. John was called to prepare the way of the Lord, to announce the wonder of a Messiah come to save his people. But

Sands of Time, Sands of Life, Tisa Muico, @tisamuico.

what did John himself know about his mission as he grew to manhood? We can sometimes assume that biblical figures lived in confidence and ease, always aware of God's will for them. But we know from Scripture that John the Baptist was not even sure that Jesus was the one for whom he was preparing the way. Had John known, he would not have sent disciples to ask Jesus if he was the one (see Mt 11:3). Certainly, he knew he was born to "go before the Lord to prepare his ways"; his own father knew this when he was born (see Lk 1:76). But did John comprehend the astonishing wonder of how exactly God would save his people? Did he know he was to announce not just the coming of a great prophet, but the coming of God-made-man?

Like John the Baptist, we have a calling from God to prepare the way of the Lord. We may wonder, "How can my calling compare to that of John the Baptist, a man who prepared the way for the Incarnate Lord?" But like John, we do not have full clarity around God's calling in our lives. John was bold and brave, but he experienced uncertainty just as we do. He only lived up to his calling because God gave him the grace. We also can be confident that, through Jesus' incarnation, life, death, and resurrection, we too have the grace to follow God's will in our lives. Of course, God does not guarantee that our way will be clear, or our lives easy and simple. But he does give us continued grace to follow him, in the Eucharist and confession especially. Even when we know how God calls us to live, many unknowns and uncertainties can lead us to feel frightened and unprepared. But like Mary, Joseph, and John the Baptist, we can radically live for heaven even when we do not know the future. Because we always have one known—Jesus Christ—the One who knows us, loves us, and calls us to prepare the way for him in our hearts.

Examen *(see p. 153)*

(see p. 153)

Heaven truly is high above and its distance from us infinite . . . But we should not be negligent or fearful on this account, as though it were impossible to reach. Rather, we should be zealous. There is no need for us to begin to [build a tower], as in the case [with the people who built the tower of Babel] . . . for their tongues were confounded, and their work was destroyed. But for us the Lord has consecrated an easy way to heaven through his Blood.

For not only has he afforded us consolation respecting the distance, but he also has come and opened the door for us that was once shut. Indeed, it was shut from the time he cast out Adam from the delight of paradise, and set the cherubim and the flaming sword, that turned every way, to keep shut the way of the tree of life—now, however, opened wide. And he that sits upon the cherubim appeared with great grace and loving kindness, having led into paradise the thief who confessed. Having entered heaven as our forerunner, he has opened the gates to all.

Paul also, "pressing toward the mark for the prize of the high calling" (Phil 3:14), was taken up to the third heaven. Then, having seen those things above and then descended, he teaches us by announcing, "For you have not come to the mount that might be touched, and that burned with fire, and clouds, and darkness, and a tempest, and to the voice of words. But you have come to Mount Sion, and unto the city of the living God, the heavenly Jerusalem, and to an innumerable company of angels, and to the general assembly and Church of the first-born, which are written in heaven" (see Heb 12:18–23). Who would not wish to enjoy the high companionship with these! Who would not desire to be enrolled with these, that he may hear with them, "Come, you blessed of my Father, inherit the kingdom prepared for you from the foundation of the world" (Mt 25:34)!

— Saint Athanasius, *Letter 43*

Journaling and Prayer

Take some time in prayer to ask the Lord what special plans he has for you. You may find that his call for you appears quite ordinary in many ways. Reflect on how God calls us to special things under the appearance of ordinariness. How does God show you his plan for you? Do you have difficulty following where God calls? Why? What is something he is calling you to consider that you have trouble accepting?

December 24

READINGS: 2 Sm 7:1–5, 8b–12, 14a, 16 / Ps 89:2–3, 4–5, 27, 29 / Lk 1:67–79

Then Zechariah his father, filled with the holy Spirit, prophesied, saying:
"Blessed be the Lord, the God of Israel,
    for he has visited and brought redemption to his people.
He has raised up a horn for our salvation
    within the house of David his servant,
even as he promised through the mouth of his holy prophets from of old:
    salvation from our enemies and from the hand of all who hate us,
to show mercy to our fathers
    and to be mindful of his holy covenant
and of the oath he swore to Abraham our father,
    and to grant us that, rescued from the hand of enemies,
without fear we might worship him in holiness and righteousness
    before him all our days.
And you, child, will be called prophet of the Most High,
    for you will go before the Lord to prepare his ways,
to give his people knowledge of salvation
    through the forgiveness of their sins,
because of the tender mercy of our God
    by which the daybreak from on high will visit us
to shine on those who sit in darkness and death's shadow,
    to guide our feet into the path of peace."

— LUKE 1:67–79

Exodus, Anna Griebe, @anna_luisamarie.

IN TODAY'S GOSPEL, WHEN Zechariah says the phrase "because of the tender mercy of our God" in reference to his son's call to prepare the way of the Lord, he is not referring to a moment in time when God decided to have compassion upon us. God did not wake up one day and suddenly realize that he wanted to have mercy on his people and save them. God never changes, so his mercy is boundless, without beginning or end. In fact, technically speaking, while in his humanity Jesus experienced the full range of human emotions, in his divinity God does not have emotions that fluctuate, dip, or flit from one feeling to another. God is Love and thus he always loves and always looks upon us with tender compassion. From the beginning of creation and in every single moment of our lives, God has loved us tenderly and desired to save us from "darkness and death's shadow" to bring us to heaven.

In heaven, we will be united with our tender, loving God. But we often forget that God also invites us to a foretaste of this heaven now. His love dwells in us through Baptism, and his tender compassion calls us in every moment, away from the fleeting pleasures and distractions of the world, to unite ourselves with him throughout our day. Our ever-growing union with God in this life prepares us for greater union with him in heaven and through it we experience our salvation now in this world. Our tender heavenly Father sent his Son to make union with him possible for us, and our lives are the context in which his graces of salvation are realized. As Advent comes to a close, we celebrate the Incarnation as the dawning of God's tender compassion on the darkness of the world and of our hearts. May this tender, enduring compassion light our way and be with us always until the end of time (see Mt 28:20).

Examen *(see p. 153)*

Oh, sublime city, send down your beams of light to these regions of darkness, this shadow of death where we still miserably live. Make our eyes so pure that, through the shining crystal of faith, they may behold the eternal good which awaits us after a short time of sacrifice and self-conquering. . . . Oh, faith, beautiful daughter of heaven, come to our souls and let us honor you; you who have enveloped us with the beautiful mantle of Baptism, and have always enriched us by means of the other sacraments! . . .

Heaven is the great prize or reward granted to good Christians, to those who are faithful to the laws of Jesus Christ! Oh, heaven! . . . To see God and to contemplate his divine beauty means to love him with the purest and most perfect love, and that love will augment in us joy and contentment and the enjoyment of our souls. Speak often of heaven to those who approach you, make them love it as well as the virtues which are required before we can be admitted to our blessed country.

— Saint Frances Xavier Cabrini, *Letter (September 1894)*

Journaling and Prayer

Saint John Vianney once asked a poor farmer in his parish who would spend hours before the tabernacle what he would say to the Lord during his long hours of prayer. The farmer replied, "I look at him, and he looks at me." Take some time beside Jesus in the manger and look at him with love. And let this little child, Love Incarnate, look back at you with love.

CHRISTMAS
December 25

VIGIL MASS: Is 62:1–5 / Ps 89:4–5, 16–17, 27, 29 / Acts 13:16–17, 22–25 / Mt 1:1–25 or 1:18–25

MIDNIGHT MASS: Is 9:1–6 / Ps 96:1–2a, 2b–3, 11–12, 13 / Ti 2:11–14 / Lk 2:1–14

DAWN MASS: Is 62:11–12 / Ps 97:1–6, 11–12 / Ti 3:4–7 / Lk 2:15–20

CHRISTMAS DAY MASS: Is 52:7–10 / Ps 98:1, 2–3a, 3b–4, 5–6 / Heb 1:1–6 / Jn 1:1–18 or 1:1–5, 9–14

In those days a decree went out from Caesar Augustus that the whole world should be enrolled. This was the first enrollment, when Quirinius was governor of Syria. So all went to be enrolled, each to his own town. And Joseph too went up from Galilee from the town of Nazareth to Judea, to the city of David that is called Bethlehem, because he was of the house and family of David, to be enrolled with Mary, his betrothed, who was with child. While they were there, the time came for her to have her child, and she gave birth to her firstborn son. She wrapped him in swaddling clothes and laid him in a manger, because there was no room for them in the inn. Now there were shepherds in that region living in the fields and keeping the night watch over their flock. The angel of the Lord appeared to them and the glory of the Lord shone around them, and they were struck with great fear. The angel said to them, "Do not be afraid; for behold, I proclaim to you good news of great joy that will be for all the people. For today in

Mother and Child, Elizabeth Zelasko, @elizabeth.zelasko.

the city of David a savior has been born for you who is Messiah and Lord. And this will be a sign for you: you will find an infant wrapped in swaddling clothes and lying in a manger." And suddenly there was a multitude of the heavenly host with the angel, praising God and saying:

> "Glory to God in the highest
> and on earth peace to those on whom his favor rests."

— Luke 2:1–14

WE ALL DESIRE THE peace that the angels proclaimed to the poor shepherds in Bethlehem at the birth of Jesus. The longing for peace is a natural movement of the human heart. But we often look for it in the wrong ways—until, through God's grace, we realize we can only find peace by embracing God's will for us—including the unexpected, which we may never have chosen for ourselves. Had Jesus not shown us the way, when we heard the angels' message of peace to those on whom God's favor rests, we might have assumed that God's favor rests on people with outward signs of wealth, attractiveness, or power. Some still suggest so. But this is false. The God-child in the manger shows us that God's favor rests on those who are like his Son—the Son of God who humbled himself to take on human form and die for our sins. The glory of God rested in this child destined for death; this child who was laid on the wood of a manger; this child who would one day be nailed to the wood of the Cross. O Divine Humility! O Divine Love!

The Son of God humbled himself to become a human child, shivering in the cold of night in an animal trough. He came in meekness and poverty to die for us. When this Infant Savior embraced death, and thus transformed it, the reality of death became shot through with the glory of God—a glory that does not die, cannot die. Indeed, the Incarnate Son of God could not die and leave death as it was. With death forever changed, we too are forever changed when we boldly enter the same downward dynamic of the Incarnation. Jesus' incarnation shows us that we can find his peace in the least likely of places. We will not find it in the accolades, worldly success, beauty, or pleasure that we seek. But we will find it in Christlike humility, poverty, and surrender. Paradoxically, we will be filled with God's glory by dying to ourselves and to all within us that is not of God. In this lifelong self-emptying, we prepare ourselves for the greatest emptying of all: death. And by embracing this dynamic of death, we find Christ and his peace. In this dynamic of death, we find heaven—eternal union with God—and receive the salvation that this tiny, divine child came to earth to bring us.

Examen *(see p. 153)*

Dearly beloved, every day and at all times the birth of our Lord and Savior from the Virgin-mother occurs to the thoughts of the faithful who meditate on divine things so that the mind may be awakened to acknowledgment of its Maker. And whether we occupy ourselves in groans of supplication, in shouts of praise, or in offering sacrifice, may we employ our spiritual insight on nothing more frequently and more trustingly than on the fact that the Son of God, begotten of the co-eternal Father, was also born by a human birth. But this Nativity, which is to be adored on heaven and earth, is suggested to us on no other day more than this day, when, while the early light still sheds its rays on nature, there is borne in upon our senses the brightness of this wondrous mystery.

For the angel Gabriel's conversation with the astonished Mary and her conceiving by the Holy Spirit as wondrously promised as believed, seem to recur not only to our memory but to our very eyes. For today the Maker of the world was born of a Virgin's womb, and he, who made all, became Son of her whom he had created. Today the Word of God appeared clothed in flesh, and that which had never been visible to human eyes began to be tangible to our hands as well. Today the shepherds learned from angels' voices that the Savior was born in the substance of our flesh and soul; and today the form of the Gospel message was prearranged by the leaders of the Lord's flocks so that we too may say with the army of the heavenly host: "Glory in the highest to God, and on earth peace to men of good will!"

— Saint Leo the Great, *Sermon 26*

Journaling and Prayer

Reflect on the paradox of the glory of God found incarnate both in a baby in a manger and in a dying man on the Cross. How do you see this paradox of life and death, power and powerlessness, and humility and glory in your life? How is God inviting you to empty yourself in imitation of the child in the manger so that you might live more fully in him and closer to heaven?

Appendix

THE *MEMENTO MORI* DAILY EXAMEN

At least once daily, cast your mind ahead to the moment of death so that you can consider the events of each day in this light.

— Saint Josemaría Escrivá

I<small>N HIS</small> R<small>ULE</small> S<small>AINT</small> Benedict urged his monks to "keep death daily before one's eyes." Benedict urged the remembrance of death so that his monks would live better in this life and keep their eyes on Jesus. Benedict also knew that the practice of remembering death is most effective when observed daily. This Advent companion will help you to begin the practice of remembering death daily, if you don't already. But Advent will eventually end and then you will have to find another way to remember death every day. For this reason, each meditation in this companion includes an *examen*, a time-honored practice that can be used to incorporate *memento mori* into your daily life.

The *examen* is a review of the day in light of God's love and mercy. Saint Ignatius of Loyola promoted the use of the *examen* to offer God praise and gratitude, identify areas of weakness in which God's help is needed, and to ask for grace for the future. This valuable spiritual practice has been encouraged in the Church for centuries because it has many benefits. The *examen* is a perfect way to incorporate *memento mori* into daily life since making an examen already implicitly evaluates the day in view of heaven. The version of the *examen* found below, however, *explicitly* incorporates *memento mori* as a step in which you review the day in the context of your final hours.

How to Make the Memento Mori Daily Examen

Step One: Become Aware of God's Presence

Close your eyes and become present to God dwelling within you through your Baptism. Imagine yourself as a child under God's omniscient, compassionate gaze. Try to visualize yourself stepping out of your self-centeredness in order to see reality through the loving eyes of God. This step is a crucial beginning to the *examen* as God's perspective on our lives is the only important one.

Step Two: Ask for the Holy Spirit's Guidance

Offer a short prayer asking the Holy Spirit to help you to see the day in the light of God's grace.

Step Three: Review the Day

Ask the questions, "How has God loved me today?" and "How have I loved God and my neighbor today?" Sometimes an obvious moment in the day will jump out—positive or negative—and you can sit with it. This step, however, is not like the examination of conscience before confession. Focusing on the negative may come more naturally, but try to note both the positive and negative events of the day and bring them before God in thanksgiving and sorrow.

Step Four: Remember Your Death

Consider the day in view of the last moments of your life. Envision your deathbed scene and subsequent judgment before Jesus. Reflect on whatever arose in the previous step in the context of eternal life. Consider the question, "If I were to die tomorrow, would I be ready to meet Jesus?" In this step, be sure to thank God for everything in the day that prepared you for heaven. Finish by asking God for the graces you need to better prepare for your death, the timing of which remains unknown.

Step Five: Look Toward Tomorrow

End by looking forward to the next day. In this step, thank God for the gift of another day of life, should it be God's will. Think of the specific events of the following day, especially those for which you need particular graces. Visualize yourself trusting and acting in God's grace as you live both the trying and joyful moments of the next day. This step, if done faithfully, will lead to concrete behavioral and emotional changes in your life.

Note: At first, the *examen* may take about ten minutes, but once you get used to the practice it can be done in less time. Do not get caught up in doing the steps precisely; there are many different ways to do the *examen*. All that matters is that you get into the rhythm and spirit of the practice and see it bearing fruit.

Let us prepare ourselves for a good death, for eternity. Let us not lose our time in lukewarmness, in negligence, in our habitual infidelities.

— Saint John Vianney

ART ACKNOWLEDGMENTS

Thank you to Sr. Danielle Victoria Lussier, FSP, and Sr. Linda Salvatore Boccia, FSP, the designers for the *memento mori* series. Sr. Danielle Victoria designed the logo and the covers for all the books in the series. She also had the inspired idea to invite other artists to contribute to this Advent Companion. I am so thankful to her for all the work she did to make that happen and to all the artists who contributed their work to make this book so much more than it would have been otherwise.

Memento mori has often centered around art and symbolism for a reason. Meditation on death needs beauty and symbol because it touches on something deeper than words. Thank you to all the following artists for giving our readers so many profound works to ponder as they meditate on their death. This book would not have been the same without you!

Sr. Theresa Aletheia Noble, FSP

The Crucified Christ, Gabrielle Schadt, @gabrielleschadt.

Erica Tighe Campbell, @beaheartdesign

Work Title: Death into New Life (p. 90)

Work Description: Little deaths happen over and over again in our lives, preparing us ultimately for our final death. These little deaths also give life to something new—a new way of seeing, a new beginning, a new lesson. The skeletons of the past fertilize the ground for new growth.

Bio: Erica Tighe Campbell is the owner and founder of Be a Heart. She spends her days mothering her young daughter, Frances, and her nights designing goods that speak to the cycle of life, death, and resurrection in our everyday lives. She lives in San Antonio with her husband, Paul.

Valerie Delgado, @pax.valerie

Work Title: You Turn Graves into Gardens (p. 124)

Work Description: Digital drawing

Bio: Valerie is an artist, dreamer, daughter of the Father, and the owner of the online shop PAX.Beloved. She is passionate about designing beautiful, relatable Catholic art that leads to the heart of the Father.

Diego Diaz, diegodiaz_gt.dribbble.com

Work Title: O Death (p. 64)

Work Description: This work is a mixed-media illustration in commemoration of Easter, portraying the words of the Scriptures on the agony of death itself. It is grounded in the First Epistle to the Corinthians, written by Saint Paul as his manifesto on Christ's victory for humanity over sin through his passion, death, and resurrection.

Bio: Diego Diaz is a Catholic communication designer and illustrator based in a little country called Guatemala. In response to a compelling need for the new evangelization in today's world and a deep thirst for self-identity and meaning, he founded his own art and design studio. He uses his work to bring light, beauty, and truth to a broken world.

Yohanes Dony, @psychedony

Work Title: Stairway to Heaven (p. 111)

Work Description: The artist's spiritual journey has been profoundly influenced by Romans 8:39, which tells us that "[nothing] will be able to separate us from the love of God in Christ Jesus our Lord." When our earthly journey is over, all we will have left will be God's love. The skull in this piece represents death, the clock represents our journey in this life, and the lilies are the beauty behind the mystery. The piece was inspired by Led Zeppelin's song "Stairway to Heaven" and its colors and composition by 1960s psychedelic poster art.

Bio: Yohanes Dony is an art enthusiast who loves to create a piece of art by combining typography with illustration.

Mary Dudek, marydudekart.com

Work Title: Catacombs (p. 167)

Work Description: This life-size ceramic skull was made for a client who wished to keep a remembrance after visiting the catacombs in Rome.

Bio: Mary Dudek is a figure sculptor and sacred fine artist from Detroit, Michigan. She is dedicated to serving God and the Church by creating beautiful figures designed to help the viewer encounter Christ.

Photo Credit: Spirit Juice

Tricia Hope Dugat, @providential_co

Work Title: Memento Mori (p. 86)

Work Description: The aesthetic of this piece is informed by the artist's childhood in the Desert Southwest and the traditions around All Souls Day. The skeletal figure is crowned with flowers that represent life and holds the hourglass as a reminder of the swift passage of time. The flowers that drop from her hands recall the words of Jesus, "Whoever loses their life for my sake will find it" (Mt 16:25). While the image reminds us of our mortality, the colorful blooms and nearby church as a sacramental refuge convey the hope of being crowned with eternal life in heaven.

Bio: Tricia Dugat is a designer/illustrator with twenty years of experience and a convert to the Catholic faith. She lives in Texas with her husband and five kiddos.

Anna Griebe, @anna_luisamarie

Work 1 Title: Vanitas (p. 102)

Work 1 Description: Woodcut and letterpress on paper

Work 2 Title: Exodus (p. 144)

Work 2 Description: Linocut on fabric with mixed media

Bio: Anna Griebe is a wife, mother, and artist. She lives with her husband and four sons on a homestead in rural Michigan. Her work reflects contemplations on the suffering and joy that she has experienced in her life thus far, while always striving to maintain sight of the eternal.

Cory and Marie Heimann, @LikableArt @fawnlyprints

Work Title: Remember Your Death (p. 38)

Work Description: Hand-lettered by Marie; photographed and styled by Cory.

Bio: Cory and Marie Heimann are a husband-and-wife creative duo. Cory is the creative director at Likable Art and Marie shares her painting and hand-lettering through her shop, Fawnly. They both desire to awaken others to see beauty, which drives their love for collaborating and creating. Cory and Marie's favorite creations are their four boys, with two babies in heaven.

Hope Helmer, @hopehelmer

Work Title: Old Church Window (p. 18)

Work Description: This photo was taken in an old church while the artist was visiting Scotland. As she walked by, the light caught her eye, and she quickly snapped the picture.

Bio: Hope Helmer is a wife and photographer located in Alberta, Canada. Inspired by her faith, she seeks to capture in her photos the beauty of Christianity: Love.

Joe Kim, @palcampaign

Work Title: Little Deaths (p. 60)

Work Description: We experience many "little deaths" throughout life that transport us to a higher plane. What is it that we need to shed? Our egos? The shame of an already reconciled sin? The pain of regret? May we allow the Master Gardener to prune all that no longer serves us.

Bio: Joe is the creativity and innovator behind PAL Campaign, an online Catholic goods shop "for future saints" based in Los Angeles, CA.

James Langley, @langley.artgram

Work 1 Title: Edith Stein (p. 30)

Work 1 Description: (Black India ink pen with Rublev watercolor on Khadi handmade cotton rag paper, 16 in. x 12 in.) I heard Truth speak when she said: "Those who remain silent are responsible." To remember her words, I wanted to make this painting of Sister Teresa Benedicta of the Cross, also known as Edith Stein.

Work 2 Title: Death of Saint Joseph (p. 120)

Work 2 Description: This drawing is a preliminary study for one wing of an oil on canvas triptych intended to envision birth, growth, and death in the life of the Holy Family of Nazareth. The finished painting hangs in a chapel at Murray Hill Place, New York City.

Bio: James Langley is a figurative painter whose work aspires to reveal immortality through the beauty of the mortal body.

Chris Lewis, @barituscatholic

Work Title: The Final Battle (p. 47)

Work Description: This work depicts a man who has fought his last battle in life and faced his mortality. He holds a sword that symbolizes the many struggles in life—particularly those against sin—and a rosary wrapped around his hand that signifies a life of piety. This final place of rest under the care of angels and beneath a stained-glass image of our Lord shows the desire to die close to the Church and the sacraments, to see our Lord in heaven. The flowers and butterflies symbolize hope in the resurrection and the glory attained after judgment: "Well done, my good and faithful servant" (Mt 25:21).

Bio: Chris Lewis is the illustrator behind BARITUS Catholic Illustration, a project devoted to creating works of art that are inspired by the rich artistic legacy of the Catholic Church and promote the good, the true, and the beautiful in a way that resonates with the faithful today.

Daniela Madriz de Quintana, @daniela.madriz.design

Work Title: Remember You're Just a Man (p. 34)

Work Description: What a joy to realize you're just human! What a gift to discover God is in charge! What a relief to surrender to his love!

Bio: Daniela is a Guatemalan independent designer focused on visual identity design. For the past seven years, her focus has been the branding of Catholic institutions and companies.

Christy Mandin, @christymandin

Work Title: Our Lady of the Lunas (p. 132)

Work Description: Luna moths are symbolic of souls and transformation, while the lily of the valley represents a return to happiness. This work reflects the artist's desire for all souls to return to happiness.

Bio: Christy is an author/illustrator of children's books and a freelance artist for major retailers. She enjoys weaving the seasonal, the spiritual, and the whimsical into the fabric of her art.

Sr. Laura Rosemarie McGowan, FSP, laurarosemarie-mcgowan.pixels.com

Work Title: Saint Michael (p. 98)

Work Description: This painting is a representation of Saint John's vision in the Book of Revelation (see Rev 12:3–10). Michael battles a great red ancient dragon known as the devil and Satan, the deceiver of the whole world. Satan is represented as larger than Michael because of his great evil. However, Michael is granted great power from God to conquer the power of evil, and the Archangel Michael continues to help us in the battle against evil.

Bio: Sr. Laura Rosemarie is a graduate of the Atelier-Lack School of Fine Arts, trained in charcoal and oil portraiture, drawing, and illustration. Born in Minneapolis, she now lives in Boston. Art is her passion. As a Daughter of St. Paul, she believes that her art becomes a channel of God's love and mercy in the world.

Photo Credit: Jake Belcher, @jakebphotog

Ryan McQuade, @ryanmcq

Work Title: On the Last Day (p. 52)

Work Description: When I thought of what the *memento mori* devotion has meant to me, I was reminded of these lines from Scripture in a song I've sung in church my whole life: "I will raise him up on the last day" (Jn 6:40). I hope that while this piece might remind you of the grave and your inevitable death, it will also assure you of your inevitable resurrection.

Bio: Ryan McQuade is a graphic designer and illustrator whose work is rooted in honesty, Catholic tradition, and a little darkness. His work explores the intersection of faith and doubt, the rich history of

Catholicism and its ability to always speak to the present culture, and the margins of the faith that we seldom explore.

Cory Mendenhall, @ForDustThouArt

Work 1 Title: Memento Mori Still Life (p. 56)
Work 1 Description: Ink and watercolor
Work 2 Title: Memento Mori Window (p. 68)
Work 2 Description: Ink and watercolor
Bio: Cory Mendenhall is an artist and illustrator living and working in Brooklyn, New York. Cory and his wife are recent converts and were welcomed into the Catholic Church at the Easter Vigil 2021. With his illustrations, Cory strives to invite viewers to contemplate life's deeper mysteries.

Harmony Miller, @hrmndesigns

Work Title: La Mort Attend (Death Awaits) (p. 82)
Work Description: This piece is inspired by how death awaits each of us. The colorful background shapes represent how life's colors follow us even after death, because our souls are attached to Christ, who is the true artist of our lives.
Bio: Harmony Miller is an abstract artist and designer from Melbourne, Australia. She founded her small business, hrmn designs (pronounced "har-man"), in 2019. She has been an artist since she could pick up a pencil and most of her work is inspired by her relationship with God. In addition to being an artist, Harmony has worked in youth ministry and has a passion to inspire others to be their best selves by discovering their God-given purpose.

Tisa Muico, @tisamuico

Work 1 Title: The Fruit of Sin (p. 14)
Work 1 Description: No matter how attractive or inviting sin may seem, the fruit of sin is still death.
Work 2 Title: Sands of Time, Sands of Life (p. 140)
Work 2 Description: This work is a reflection on life's passing nature and the Eucharist, which is both the source and summit of our Christian life.
Bio: Tisa is the artist behind Friends in High Places, a small business she co-owns with her husband, Kevin, built around their friendship with

the saints. She and Kevin live in Calgary, Alberta, and are currently serving as the Singles for Christ Regional Couple Coordinator for Africa.

David Noble, @ignoble_one

Work Title: Heavenly Stems and Earthly Branches (p. 112)

Work Description: This depiction of death was made in response to the slow passing of the artist's friend, Nancy Rhodes. Moved by the humor and grace she showed amid intense suffering, he aimed to honor Nancy by conveying some of the peace and love that characterized her final months. The content and format are informed by Orthodox iconography and visionary, folk, and psychedelic art. The image contains multiple symbolic references to death, resurrection, and transition.

Bio: David Noble is an artist and manual laborer whose process-driven paper weavings and detailed collages are painstakingly and organically constructed over long periods of time with little to no planning. After a few close encounters with death and the loss of several friends, David rediscovered art's therapeutic benefits. Currently living in Lawrence, Kansas, he continues to create as a means of self-discovery, catharsis, and reflection.

Jay Parnell, jayparnell.com

Work Title: The Humbling (p. 81)

Work Description: (Oil on wood panel, 24 in. x 18 in., 2021) The idea behind this image is man attempting to humble himself before God. Our goal in this life is to become saints. Without this foundational virtue that goal will be elusive.

Bio: Jay Parnell is a self-taught artist based in Indianapolis, Indiana. Parnell has a background in photography and illustration but is currently working with oil paint. His narrative portraits and landscapes can be found in collections in the United States, Europe, and the Caribbean.

Photo Credit: Christopher Newell

Michelle Arnold Paine, @paine.michelle

Work Title: Mary the Chalice (p. 26)

Work Description: (Oil on panel, 30 in. x 21 in.) The inspiration for the painting comes from a line in the Marian hymn, "Mary the Dawn." As the chalice is the vessel that carries the consecrated wine (Christ's saving

Blood) to us in Communion, Mary is the container, the chalice, through which the Father chose to give us the Savior of the world.

Bio: Michelle Arnold Paine began to explore the visual richness of Catholicism while studying in Italy. She was received into full communion with the Catholic Church at Easter 2001 in the Cathedral of Orvieto, Italy. Michelle now works in Ohio with her husband and two daughters. Her paintings have been exhibited across the United States and featured in publications such as *Dappled Things*, *Ruminate Magazine*, *Christianity Today*, and *Evangelization and Culture*.

Gabrielle Schadt, @gabrielleschadt

Work Title: The Crucified Christ (p. 156)

Work Description: (Oil on Canvas, 2021) A particular passage in the Gospel of Luke touches me greatly: "This is my body, which will be given for you" (Lk 22:19). When contemplating this gift of Christ, I am overtaken by his complete and total self-giving love, and in response I wish to live out of love and make of my life and art a song of praise and thanksgiving to our Lord who has given me everything through his sacrifice on the Cross.

Bio: Gabrielle wishes to share the massive joy and love of the Lord Jesus through her work. Seeing art as a gift and reflection of infinite beauty itself, Gabrielle shares the discoveries associated with art by teaching and completing commissions out of her studio in the Quad Cities. "I believe that by creating, one gives life. I desire that art be a light that penetrates the darkest parts of the soul, to illuminate and infuse hope where hope is absent."

Jeremy Stout, @jstoutillustration

Work Title: After That Comes Judgment (p. 116)

Work Description: This work is based on Hebrews 9:27: "And just as it is appointed for man to die once, and after that comes judgment." This concept is central to the need for proclaiming the Gospel because when it's all over—it isn't over.

Bio: Jeremy Stout is a freelance illustrator living in Elkhart, Indiana, with his wife and three children. His daily goal is to love people, drink coffee, listen to metal, and draw pictures—in no particular order, but all to the glory of God.

Arienda Tankou, @thegoodsheperd_illustrations

Work Title: Memento Mori (p. 13)

Work Description: In this image we can see the penitent Mary Magdalene meditating upon a skull—the symbol of the shortness of the time that we have on earth, but also a remembrance of the illusory vanities that can entangle us on our way. "Vanity of vanities, says Qoheleth, vanity of vanities! All things are vanity" (Eccl 1:2).

Bio: Arienda is a young artist living in France. Using pencils and ink, she draws images of faith, trying to catch glimpses of God's grace and love on paper.

Kreg Yingst, @psalmprayers

Work Title: Morire a se stessi (Die to Self) (p. 94)

Work Description: This block print, depicting Saint Francis and Sister Death, is from a series of visual meditations on the life of Saint Francis. Long before his physical death, Saint Francis suffered a lifelong spiritual dying to self—not all at once, but moment by moment, event by event, through his actions and his words. "Be praised, my Lord, through our Sister Bodily Death, from whose embrace no living person can escape" (Saint Francis of Assisi, "Canticle of the Sun").

Bio: Kreg Yingst received his BA in studio art from Trinity University in San Antonio (1983) and his MA in painting from Eastern Illinois University (1996). He taught art for thirteen years and has been a full-time artist since 2003. Both a painter and a self-taught printmaker, he develops his work from an idea-based or narrative concept.

Elizabeth Zelasko, @elizabeth.zelasko

Work 1 Title: Burning Bush (p. 128)

Work 1 Description: A tradition links Mary to the burning bush in the story of Moses. The bush was burning but not consumed by the flames. Mary contains in her womb that which even the cosmos cannot contain, and yet she is not consumed or overtaken by it. Here, Christ and the cosmos are contained in her womb in an icon style referred to as "Our Lady of the Sign."

Work 2 Title: Mother and Child (p. 148)

Work 2 Description: I adore capturing quiet moments in art. William Bouguereau was king of quiet moments. I completed this drawing of

Bouguereau's painting while my own child was about the same age as the infant Jesus. What a gift to be able to meditate on these passing moments.

Bio: Elizabeth studied fine art at the School of Visual Arts in Manhattan before attending the Prosopon School of Iconology, where she studied traditional Russian Orthodox iconography; then she finished her Bachelor of Fine Arts degree at Rocky Mountain College of Art and Design. Elizabeth creates commissioned pieces for Catholic publishers and institutions, as well as private individuals. She also gives talks on the theological aspects and material processes of creating traditional icons.

Catacombs, Mary Dudek, marydudekart.com.

BOOKS & MEDIA

The Daughters of St. Paul operate book and media centers at the following addresses. Visit, call, or write the one nearest you today, or find us at www.paulinestore.org

CALIFORNIA

| 3908 Sepulveda Blvd, Culver City, CA 90230 | 310-397-8676 |
| 3250 Middlefield Road, Menlo Park, CA 94025 | 650-562-7060 |

FLORIDA

| 145 S.W. 107th Avenue, Miami, FL 33174 | 305-559-6715 |

HAWAII

| 1143 Bishop Street, Honolulu, HI 96813 | 808-521-2731 |

ILLINOIS

| 172 North Michigan Avenue, Chicago, IL 60601 | 312-346-4228 |

LOUISIANA

| 4403 Veterans Memorial Blvd, Metairie, LA 70006 | 504-887-7631 |

MASSACHUSETTS

| 885 Providence Hwy, Dedham, MA 02026 | 781-326-5385 |

MISSOURI

| 9804 Watson Road, St. Louis, MO 63126 | 314-965-3512 |

NEW YORK

| 115 E. 29th Street, New York City, NY 10016 | 212-754-1110 |

SOUTH CAROLINA

| 243 King Street, Charleston, SC 29401 | 843-577-0175 |

VIRGINIA

| 1025 King Street, Alexandria, VA 22314 | 703-549-3806 |

CANADA

| 3022 Dufferin Street, Toronto, ON M6B 3T5 | 416-781-9131 |